INEXORABLE

The Struggles and Mental Shifts in the
Persistent Search for Meaning in the Life of
an Air Steward

LIN C H

ISBN: 1516983947
ISBN-13: 978-1516983940

Author: Lin C H

Book Publication Date: November 1, 2014

Inexorable
ISBN-10: 1516983947
ISBN-13: 978-1516983940

Printed in the United States of America

This book is dedicated to anyone whose mind is torn into two or more parts

LIN C H

Preface

Truth is a difficult subject to handle, yet how can we find it with the ever-fluctuating states of mind we live with, which have an indirect but nevertheless, huge influence on the result of any inquiry. Which state of mind is best suited to find the slippery truth?

Is there such a thing as truth? Do efforts to find it distort our perception of it? Does knowing the truth change it? If the truth is somewhere, can we ever find it? Can we use methods available to humans to find it? In fact, do we need to find it? And why are we so interested in it?

Many people and groups have sworn by their version of the absolute Truth, but is anyone really telling it? Can we be sure the person claiming to know it, is not swayed by factors other than the truth when he or she tells it? Pressure may be applied to ensure social harmony or to cause disruption, and special interests may make someone swear they are espousing the truth when they did not. Truth could then be twisted to coalesce with the current agenda, and a school of thought favoured for the social and material benefits the teller gets.

Does the person who talks about the truth know it at all? Many factors influence and distort one's perception though he or she would probably deny it. Money or name affects judgment and flow of ideas, as do the perceived consequences of assuming a belief. Personal psychological needs are usually addressed at this time. As the person searches for truth, is the mental state stressed by particular events or affected by the environment? How does one handle issues affecting the person, and is the truth compromised in the handling process? Has the discerning mind been influenced by substances consumed – or exposed to them in other ways? Yet if the mind is clear of influences, does it mean it would have found the truth? Can one ever be completely free of influences?

Against this backdrop of perennial difficulties, how does a person's life affect the search for the truth? How does the search affect one's life in the atmosphere of constant stress and change related to certain occupations?

I have written the story of someone caught up in this search, while engaged in one of the most disruptive occupations of modern times, a flight steward with the world's most challenging airline, flying into different time zones as he squeezes into different schedules and faces various types of people. In the process, I created characters and circumstances that are as close to reality as is possible.

Throughout the book, the protagonist has to cope with his changing moods and shifting states of being. I tried to reflect this tendency as best as I could. Different writing styles are adopted in certain chapters to further this end.

There are different ways to read a book. This book was designed to be read from the beginning, but each chapter can also be enjoyed by itself without the understanding of it being compromised.

INEXORABLE

CONTENTS
(PAGES ARE ACCURATE IN THE PRINTED VERSION)

Chapter 1

1979: Ambivalent

I first met Feng Ren on a long trip when he had told the Purser he was high-handed, stubborn and uncommunicative. That was in front of all eighteen crew members. Since then, I often heard the word "Professor" whenever Feng Ren was around, or he was a subject of discussion.

On this flight, my first as a Junior Purser (JP) and my second with Feng Ren – after we completed meal service – when I asked the more experienced man why they were calling him "Professor", the flutter in my stomach reminded me I knew the answer. Feng admitted readily the title was really a form of ridicule for him. Then good-naturedly, he told me what he had been through. His sincerity and openness were obvious as he exhorted me to be strong and intelligent.

I decided he would be a good companion for the rest of the long tour of duty, to talk to about my problems. Feng is fresh air, so different from the shallowness permeating the entire atmosphere.

***

Something happened to me through the years. My thoughts have changed focus. I've metamorphosed from being obsessed only with the meaning of existence to someone who worries just about everything. Now I see everything is linked in a complicated web of existence. Everything is cause and effect, and every effect in turn causes another effect. Aside from the direct effect, there are rippling effects; interchangeable effects.

Just now, in my room, I was afraid my hand became dirty. When I wiped it with a tissue, it seemed the area was still dirty. Then I wiped it again and worried some tissue fibres were left on the hand. I didn't believe it was true, but as I looked at the spot on my hand, I was almost sure they were there and suddenly, I saw clearly two strands of fibre. I couldn't deny it anymore. What should I do? If I wiped my hand with a dry cloth, it might also leave fibres. If I wiped with a wet cloth, my hand would be wet, and there would be a wet towel in the toilet. I decided to blow away the fibres.

After doing so, I was relieved. But as I was about to put on my shoes, I realised my hand was stained with saliva. In desperation, I tried to forget the problem by focusing on the chore of putting on my shoes. My hand touched the sole! Why was I so careless to have touched something dirty? I walked out of my room and forced this issue out of my mind.

But those thoughts: they left me, only to return; they left again, and returned again.

***

I will be late again for an appointment, this time by ten minutes. I'm meeting Feng in the unremarkable hotel lobby. I regret this thing should have been the cause again, but there were worse occasions.

He walks towards me and stretches out his hand. I shake it. It has the firmness of a purposeful wise man, yet he is a mere airline steward. His large oriental eyes are radiant even after the long tiring flight, but I'm not surprised. I've come to think, he could be a superman, full of spirit and energy at all times. He is someone who doesn't feel tired, or get into depression. Tucked below black eyebrows and thick hair combed simply to the sides, fearless eyes gleam steadily.

He ventures. "I know this place. If you don't mind it, we go there. Chicken curry with rice and vegetables: delicious but only six hundred yen. Don't be stingy with food, but we also have to spend within our means. We must save for the future. Confucius teaches that."

"It's okay. Sounds reasonable."

"When was the last time we flew together?"

"Last year, when you were already a JP. Ali *Botak* called for debriefing after the flight. You told that tyrant off. Really great! Everyone was shocked. No one dares defy a senior. But you did it even to Ali."

We walk out of the warm stifling hotel into the airy Tokyo night. It's dotted with bright lights: stationary and steady at lamp posts, buildings and skies; shifty and jerky when they move about on rumbling vehicles. We're wearing the dark-blue company-issued overcoats over layers of shirts and trousers. A wind freezes up our faces and stiffens our hands. Feng, looking somewhat spiritual, is slightly shorter than me, has average height, and a gait which is purposeful.

"We've to stand up against bullies. The world is now democratic. Ali's style is obsolete. He asked for it. He said we could speak our mind. Everyone heard. So, I took the opportunity to give it to him. He could not answer and told me to sit down. In other words: shut up!"

"Let me come to the point," I say unsteadily. "You look like an intelligent guy who can be trusted. I need your help."

"Tell me your problem. Everything can be solved."

"You're an optimist."

"You've to be an optimist. Never say "die". When I was young, my father called me useless. I don't blame him. You see, he was uneducated. He thought by saying that, I would improve. But there was nothing wrong with me, basically. Many people treated this way went astray. Luckily, I'm different. We know now that people need to be praised. So long as someone has the right attitude, find something to praise the person with. I do that all the time, and they get motivated. However, I met people in this airline who wanted me dead. And they were educated people."

"They only wanted to kill your soul. That's worse than death."

"I'm a fighter to the end. I exercise in my room every day, or I run. I educate myself by reading a lot. I took courses. I save money, and I bought a HDB flat. Today, it's worth two times what I paid five years ago, and I'm still staying there. I told my brother to buy one too. He took my advice. Today, his flat is worth as much as mine, and he has one son. A daughter is on the way. Yet, after my father died, he was drinking and gambling. I am not boasting. I only want to educate people."

"You're honourable!"

"My other brother: he is in uni now and since I can afford it, I am paying for his education. When it comes to education, it's a must. It is the one thing you should give, especially when the person is family. Confucius teaches study is very important. I read philosophy books. I learn from those great men. I love people. I love my family. The family always comes first, for me. You can't control the world but try to cultivate your family; try to influence the world for good. I don't mind people taking advantage of me. But if there is bad intention; at a certain stage, I will fight, though in the end I always forgive and forget."

I interrupt: "Being selfless, you lose a lot."

He listens and says, "Love keeps me going. I am selfless because I love. I am kind and mean, but when I'm mean, it is for the good. You must have heard! Spare the rod and spoil the child!"

***

We walk through the old (and mildewed) entrance of Tokyo Station, hands pushed deep into our pockets. A few metres away is a simple old restaurant. Once inside the uncrowded place, heating "thaws" out my body.

We sit at a table. A plain-looking Japanese girl in a simple dress approaches and greets in Japanese. Feng points outside, and the smiling girl nods immediately. We follow her out of the restaurant. In the cold, Feng points at a tray laid with a plate of mock chicken curry and rice, and a bowl of salad in the window display. I point to a *bento* box, the respective compartments filled with plastic tempura, salad and soba. Then we scamper back into the warmth of the restaurant.

I'm a voracious eater. Still, I am thin. All my energy somehow dissipates quickly into the void. I'm always in a state of angst, or what some say incurable doubt. How I wish I'm normal like Feng! When something happens or someone speaks, he understands straightaway and is able to respond. He doesn't get confused, he knows what to do or say, and he does not keep changing his mind. Even if he is wrong, he believes he's right. He is happy enough, he is active mostly, he never needs so much food, and he has normal weight.

The same waitress comes with a jug, heavy with water inside. It's wet outside with condensation. She holds a towel against the base to absorb the dripping moisture. We take two glasses from the tray on the centre of our table and sit them upright. Feng looks at her intently and praises her looks in English. She doesn't look pretty to me, in any way. Does she understand a little English? All the same, she says, "*Domo arigato*", bows and giggles. She pours the iced water into the two glasses and scurries away.

"These girls are what I mean. They are proud of what they do, and they do it well. It can be a simple thing, like serving customers. If they like you, they let you fuck, and they fuck you. I fucked a few like them. When they enjoyed it, they thanked me and gave me tokens of appreciation. They are sincere. I gave them what they wanted in return, in the best possible way. That's what I call meaning and love."

I remind him I have a problem.

"Tell me about it."

"You won't tell anyone?"

"Trust me. When I say something, I mean it. Of course, I can also change my mind because I'm free. But I don't change my mind anyhow. Only when I have to kill, I kill."

He lowers his determined forehead. He looks at me with unyielding eyes and stiffens his body. Then he curls his lips, stifles a yell and performs a karate chop in the air. He looks like a samurai on Japanese television, a defender of the weak. He is a fighter for justice, one who solves problems and clears minds. He is a teacher of optimism and humanism. Maybe, he is enlightened. I'm sure I can trust him.

I tell him what happened in my room before we met in the lobby. But after I finished talking, I remember something else.

"It's more than that. When I try to tackle the issue, I've not used the time to do what is the best for myself. Surely, that affects not only me, but also the hand. In fact, I'm not using my attention and energy in the best possible way for the affected hand; not even to the extent of what I would normally have done. And to be agitated about it makes it worse, but I'm agitated. The more I try not to, the more I am. This series of events started from that moment in my room."

An uncomfortable lump forms in my throat as I continue, "What I do and how I do it, is affecting the hand. What I don't do has a different outcome. When I think, how I think, how long I take to think: these have consequences on my hand. How I feel is also very important and affects what I do. Frankly, I don't know what to do."

Then I remember a problem. In dismay, I say: "I can try to make up what I owe myself and my hand. But I can't see how I could find equally inclined conditions inside me, if I can't have better or optimal ones to work in. And how long do I wait for external circumstances which are as supportive as those moments in my room (had I stayed!) to now, if I can't get something better? And when the moment comes (if it comes), I would probably have forgotten what I've to do."

"Forget such things. Just do whatever you have to and things will flow along," Feng says forcefully.

I knew he was going to say that. I'm not sure I should be disappointed with him. "You mean you don't bother about the truth. You close your eyes and just flow … . Do you believe in God?"

"I know there is God, but who cares! Everything worth doing in this world is for humans, like you and me."

"I've come to be psychoanalysed."

"I just told you. Be yourself. Don't look for happiness; the more you look for it, the more you can't find it. Make friends, help them, love them, but don't be afraid to be cruel in order to be kind. Remember the kung fu hero. He only cares for what's right. Remove evil, finish up enemies if you have to. Slaughter negative thoughts!"

I am trembling with excitement and the angst.

"I love your attitude and your adventures, but I can't live like you. You are very sure, but I've many doubts. I doubt my existence, I doubt God, I doubt good and bad. I doubt everything."

***

The waitress brings Feng his tray, bows and scurries away. I'm glad he scoops the curry onto his rice and eats. There is no need to wait for me or to give excuses. Man-made hypocrisy wastes time and distracts. They're for people who have little to occupy themselves with or don't know what life is. He is enjoying his food, and he's in control. He seems natural.

She comes and places my box neatly in front of me. She takes the lid, and bows politely before she walks away. The hot, golden items smell inviting.

My chopsticks pick the crispy battered prawn and lift it to my mouth. The tempura stops at the entrance, and I push it in. Despite its tastiness, I chew with much effort. I gulp it down with water.

"I am jammed. I'm always caught in this sort of dilemma. I want to do something, but I'm stopped from being spontaneous. I ate the prawn, but knew it also dirtied my hand and the areas outside my lips."

"Look, do what you want to do and the hell with other things."

"But contradictions like this mean a lot. And what happens if the overall results are worse than what I hope for?"

"Fuck them!"

"I dropped problems before. After a while, I found I couldn't continue to do so. Then I managed to tell them to fuck off, but soon they were unwilling too."

"When I'm stuck like this: sometimes, I punch the walls, I kick the pillow. Harmless things! Just don't be afraid!"

"I tried those too!"

"Keep trying till you succeed."

I say, "I am not afraid. I'm only afraid of myself because I don't know when it'll come. Sometimes, it waits there even before the beginning, sometimes it appears almost at the end. Sometimes, it creeps in, in the middle of something."

His eyes focus and search my face as I continue. "What if I can't think 'to hell with other things'? What if I don't get positive postulates or helping thoughts?"

I don't know what I am talking about. A hundred ideas hit my head, making the world flip and turn. I hear him rattling on. I've lost control again.

"Can you return to where I stopped and start from there again?" But I can't concentrate and can't remember where I stopped. Even if he remembers where it was and restarts from there, it would be useless because I won't know whether he has got it right.

I've no choice, but to wait for another opportunity to begin such a conversation again. Perhaps, I will begin all over or start at the right point where I give him the perfect problem and see how he solve it. This will cost me something in many ways, but what can I do? He seems to be talking about Ali now, but I'm not sure. Then, it becomes something else. I hear sounds, and when I try to know what they mean, they remain sounds, which jam my mind and move heavily.

"... meet people ... for travels ... adventures ... see things differently even before you finish ... married ... children are good for the soul ... makes a man complete. ..."

He is still talking: "Be simple ... sincere ..."

I'm not sure I understand what he says.

"I know all this," I protest. "But there is no end."

"You ... stop somewhere. ..."

"I've thought about everything ... I can't do everything ... anything ... ." Anger builds up further, squeezing my voice box. I cough out the words: "Nothing helped ultimately. ..."

"When ... want to do anything ... you've to mean it. ..."

"I know ..."

I realise he has finished his meal. Only brownish stains remain on his empty plate. In his salad bowl, three shreds of green cabbage covered in mauve dressing stare back at me. I've to finish my meal too. I do my part. I feel the delight I should be having as I chew and swallow my juicy food – but I don't enjoy it!

Chapter 2
Off Day

Last night, we returned to the hotel after dinner. Feng asked if I would like to join him in the Crew Room for a hot drink and chitchat. I would've agreed to do so if I wasn't so tired. My tiredness was not due to the day's work. I had to get to my room to be alone.

I regret what happened. Why couldn't I pull myself from the brink? Why did I allow those thoughts to take me away from what Feng was saying? Did I miss something important? Or, had I lost something? Now, I've to wait till tomorrow to talk to Feng, and who knows if it would even take place. After all, we will be on standby tomorrow.

And after making a mistake, why didn't I recover and return to what Feng was saying? This wasn't difficult, yet the same mistake kept repeating itself though I promised myself each time it happened, it would be the last. I shouldn't drive myself into more frenzy. I would only suffer more – and make things worse. This has been proved many times before, yet I can never remember if it's really true.

***

He is leaving his room at eleven to meet a friend (a woman) for lunch and if things go well, he would only be available tomorrow. He told me he always treats his women well and gives them room to think. If at the end, he and a woman get married, it would be a blessing for both of them.

He should be leaving in thirty minutes. I don't think I should see him before he leaves. Today, I've all the time in the world to myself, yet I don't know what to do with it. Or rather, I don't know whether to do anything with it. I'm a long way from even basic understanding which I need to have before anything can be meaningful.

I know I won't get the answer today. I am pessimistic I will ever find the answer even after a long time. I'm not optimistic I will find the answer at all. I am inclined to think (whether I'm really here or not), that I don't have a valid reason to exist. There are twelve more days before I get home and do something I like, but then what? Before long, I would've realised again that the problem remains.

I'm extremely bored. I had continued sleeping as much as I could after I woke up to avoid that feeling. I can't sleep anymore. I can call up some crew members if they're still in the hotel, but I value my freedom. I've to be what I am, to think when I want to. Otherwise, it feels like something isn't right. What follows would be something different. With Feng, it's all right because he understands all this. He is always ready to listen. And he has pearls of wisdom to be tapped.

Still, this boredom is better than that thing which exists in the front of my head after growing at the back. Sometimes, it crouches in a dark corner in front to wait. At other times, it enlarges quietly behind a wall. Once it pounces, it drags me somewhere, and I can't find my way back. I held it by the ears many times before to analyse it, but I can't remember being successful in controlling it.

At the end, I'm somehow controlled by it. It rarely gives blinding insight though I do get exuberance from it. Desperation is normal with the thing which, most of the time, tears me apart. When I try to stifle it, it never works. It's locked in my head, once I remember I tried, but it hadn't worked. It comes and goes so often I normally don't notice it.

I yawn again in relief, this time bringing copious tears. Outside, the sun is shining. People are in great spirits. They don't need overcoats today. I put on warm clothes and leave my room. Heavy legs carry me out of the brownness of the hotel. I don't know where to go.

The Tokyo downtown is still a strange place to me, but I don't want to ask for help. I turn right and walk aimlessly on the pavement alongside the thoroughfare. Everywhere is people who are small, trim, energetic and move briskly. The women look alike. The men, uniformed in their dark jackets and ties, look business-like and glum.

***

I arrive at the busy Tokyo Station. Taxis in a long queue take turns to pick waiting passengers standing in a long line. This must be the main entrance. But my feeling stops here and couldn't go on to establish some form of certainty. The mind won't get on the next step! I find it impossible to decide whether I want to enter the station, or whether I should do so, so I continue walking where the straight road leads me. I realise I probably want to eat, and tell myself, consciously, to look out for suitable restaurants.

I'm in the middle of a wide, grey road with lush greenery and beautiful buildings. Stylish people, dressed in all their finery, behave with etiquette and dignity. Everything here is done with moderate ostentation. This must be the Ginza. As I walk further, I find myself in a fairyland. Even more tall, imposing buildings with bright and clear pastel colours! The road here appears to be paved with gold. Nothing appears dirty even when it is so. It is unreal. It's like a dream. I am stuck in a beautiful movie floating across a wide screen.

The pain inside reminds me it's not real.

If I am careful with what I choose to eat in the most expensive place on earth, I should have enough money to last the trip. After all, I'm paid fifty-one dollars a day. That's twenty-three American dollars. My lodging is paid for, and buses bring the crew to and from airports. The prices below those pictures in the window displays, and on the menus resting on stands are pretty standard, unless I go to one of those rare, even higher-end restaurants.

I will limit myself to just one plate of spaghetti in this exquisite restaurant in front of me, though I'm tempted to splurge now and think about it later. I am glad I don't have to tip in Japan or pay for water.

***

I follow the young and pretty waitress to the table at the end of the restaurant. The couple seated on my left is familiar, especially the man. I realise with a jolt, he is Howard Soh, the Purser, with a fashionable young girl. If I turn back now, they will notice me. I decide quickly and sit with my back towards them.

Removed from thoughts, I see their clear images in the spotless rectangular mirrors facing me. I can see what they do when I concentrate in one of those well-polished panels. I don't think they will notice me if I don't do anything that attracts attention.

The waitress is back! I point at a greenish picture on the glossy menu. She nods, bows and walks away.

In the mirror, three tables away, is Howard Soh. The girl is Chinese too. She is beautiful and looks sophisticated. I can hear them speaking Mandarin and the English practised in the island I come from, with the flat accent. Howard is in his forties and undoubtedly handsome. Tall and well-built, he wears an elegant jacket with a bow tie, and looks like Chow Yun-Fat, the suave actor. On his right, a familiar looking bottle of Hennessy XO sits on the table. Inside me, heaviness weighs down my congested heart.

My eyes examine their square table. Coffee cups and praline wrappers on the embroidered place mats show the main meals have been eaten. Outside those mats, the tablecloth reveals well-blended colours. Shining chandeliers with myriads of crystals dangle from the frescoed ceiling, while painted pictures of delicious Italian foods decorate the walls.

Howard gives the girl a cigarette and dangles one between his own lips. The girl takes the golden lighter at the side of the table, lights Howard's cigarette, and then her own. Her diamond rings sparkle on one of her fingers.

"When you close that deal in LA, remember to get me the chocolates." Her breathy stilted voice, toned by cigarette smoke, is sexy and glamorous. "It's very expensive but worth every cent. By the way, how much is the deal worth? Okay, (don't ask), but I'm sure this is another very big one. Later, in your room, we drink to your success. With that first-class cognac you bought me!"

Howard takes a moment to think. "*Aiyah*, no problem! If I can make you the happiest person in the world, why not! On your flight home, where are you working in?"

"First Class! We don't rotate positions across classes. Those who work in First Class are designated, unlike the airline from our island." She turns her face from the smoke to breathe fresher air. "I dine in Ginza five times a year. I love the ice-cream crepe and service in that restaurant. We go there later, okay? It's the best in the world, and very expensive. This restaurant is beautiful, but once you see that one, you know this is nothing."

I pull my mind together with much effort. I ask like a fisherman drawing in his heavy net: *if this restaurant is not unreal enough, where shall I go?*

I realise Howard is pretending to be a big-time businessman. Maybe, he really enjoys his make-believe, and it makes no difference whether something is real or fake. Maybe, his goal is getting pleasure from sex. Or, all he wants is to conquer and cheat a difficult girl. I'm sad for the innocent girl. I want to tell her about Howard: that his bottle is stolen from the aircraft. But she is acting too!

I don't feel like doing anything. I should let her imagine her exalted status a little longer. The trouble is I'm not enjoying this spectacle either. If Howard sees me, I would also lose my hard-to-find solitude. I want to leave, but the waitress has taken the order. Hopefully, the food hasn't been prepared! However, I would have to ask that question using gestures and drawings. Then the food comes, and I'm relieved I don't have to decide anymore.

Now, I have to eat. The food tastes bland. I'm paying a lot and spending time on it, only to have bland food again.

I've achieved nothing. In fact, I lost again. I feel I've only been losing since that time, quite long ago. Nowadays, I can only lose. I wish the waitress hadn't come! The world outside is bright and beautiful, full of adventures and excitement, but I am tossing on a spit here.

I stand and leave my food half-eaten. I try to sit back, but I have to go. I pay at the counter by the door in a daze. I walk out of the restaurant and feel destruction tearing around me because the mistakes were unnecessary. The catastrophe will only get worse and lead to more catastrophes.

Where shall I go? I try to take control of myself, and walk back the way I came from. I feel safer this way. I'm in no mood to risk getting lost.

***

"Good morning, Mr Liu."

I look. The world has shrunk! There is no doubt this time, it's smaller. Even overseas, I am meeting colleagues and people from the small island.

The steward on training is smiling at me with the respect and admiration a senior crew member expects. His dark charming eyes is wide open like a schoolboy's. The rawness of his emotions soothes my mind. On his second supernumerary (SNY) flight, this medium-built guy is genuinely happy to see me. The novice is very down-to-earth. He dresses like someone where we come from, who buys clothes from neighbourhood shops there. He looks bulgy because of the layers of clothes beneath his sweater, while his trouser legs are wide and flared. He would look different when he has saved enough money to visit Gucci shops and carry LV bags – in less than a year.

"Hi Roland. It's past noon. And why don't you simply call me Liu!"

"Sorry Liu! I thought it is still morning," he says in Mandarin. He looks apologetic and nods the way Chinese people do. His oiled hair is neatly combed. "I slept from last night till ten-thirty this morning. Now I know why crew members have good lives. Can you tell me where the crew joint to go for lunch is? Or anywhere cheap?" The dark-yellow teeth stains make me think he hasn't begun to make free visits to the Company's dentists.

"I had fettuccine," I answer in Mandarin – the word *fettuccine* in English, since I don't know the Chinese word for it. "No, not that restaurant. Where's the other SNY?"

***

He switches back to English, sounding like a car going through a bend. "She is my batch girl. This morning she called me, but I still sleeping. I never been to a foreign country. My first SNY was Jakarta turnaround, so I only saw the airport. I saw some crew at the lobby just now, all so well-dressed up like film stars."

"You should've joined them," I said lifelessly.

"I think better not *lah*. I don't know them well. I scared of them. My batch girl cried in the toilet, that day, after she got 'zapped'. She didn't introduce to Zaiton."

"Can she work?"

"She never lifted her fingers before joined the airline. Men did anything for her. She was a model before."

A teenage girl with rosy cheeks and hair tied neatly into double buns walks by with a Cocker Spaniel. Roland beams as he stares at the young dog prancing around. Its silky brown fur gleams outside a sparkling red vest worn around its torso.

"Her life will be hell. She has to work hard, and the crew has to like her. She has to be humble when she is new. Sugar daddies can't protect her when they are always far away."

"Flying is so stressful, but no problem: I will be strong."

"Crew members make life difficult for each other. You've to kowtow to your seniors. In turn, juniors play out seniors when they get a chance."

"Yes sir!" Roland straightens and looks at his body self-consciously. "During our first SNY together, a senior steward introduced himself to her, but you know what? She stretched out her hand like Marilyn Monroe. The steward walked off straightaway."

He's getting too chatty for me. I'm no longer listening as we stand there. I scan the people passing by but notice nothing. The blotches of colours and the hurrying shapes make me giddy. I want to tell him I have to go, but I can't make myself do so. I remember clearly I didn't have a good time when I was alone earlier.

"I heard some of our girls are really beautiful."

"Yes …" I persevere. I remind myself there is really nothing else I like to do.

"There is one hostess in our Company, right? She refused to be the concubine of the world's richest sultan. He is ugly, but other girls will jump for his money. But another girl became mistress to the Malaysian Beer King. Smart, very lucky girl! The *Dato* treats her very well."

"True!"

"I have to tell you I am so happy. I applied to be a steward many times, but didn't even get one interview. Then I joined as internal staff and applied again. At last, I flying with this airline. I am forever grateful to this Company. I will work very hard and make passengers happy." He stops talking to catch his breath. "I going to save money. I am already old, *lah*. I know one steward; he bought a house after just three years flying. He eats on board and buys 'dry stores' to bring overseas. He cooks in his hotel room. Like that, he does not miss mother's foods. His combs, razors, writing materials, all free. His shampoos and his bath soaps, and toilet paper provided by the hotels. When he is on holiday, he gets free tickets, and he stays with the crew."

"Some crew members carry a kitchen when they fly. But they gamble away the money saved, buy expensive stuff, or waste it on women."

"I want to buy a cooker in Akihabara. It is cheaper in Japan because it is made here. The pot very good for cooking in the room lah. You get sacked if they catch you *ala* 'squatting' lah. I want to buy a Rolex next year." He lifts his sleeve to show his flaking Seiko.

"Hah? …"

"I see you don't have expensive tastes. By the way, how many steps are on the staircase to the upper deck?"

"I don't know."

"It is OK. I don't think any of you will ask me that question. You guys look quite nice lah. I have to go. A lot to do."

I'm neither relieved nor sad he is going. I look at my watch. 14:00 on the digital face! I add one hour to the Casio. 15:00 is three in the afternoon in Tokyo. My lifeless legs drag an unsettled body towards my hotel.

***

I'm a foreigner and a stranger, and the folks around leave me alone. Yet, I don't have the feeling of being cast aside because this is a reticent country. I'm happy with that, except those bodies carry the heavy burden of an inscrutable purpose and rush about in madness to accomplish some odd mission.

A hot current of desperation burns through my being. These people irritate me to the core, I realise. I want to scream at them as I would if I'm still by myself in my room. I must do what I really want.

I pass Tokyo Station as its rushing anxious crowds make me angrier. The colourful restaurant on my left, displaying dummy foods, looks familiar. It's larger than most other restaurants that sell ramen and *gyoza* dumplings. I've walked past the three-storey whitewashed building where the restaurant is situated.

But the rare sight of a grimy old man in dirty clothes, now sits on the long bench on the side of the pavement in front of the building. His long dirty hair is matted, and he smells like he has been sleeping in subways and didn't bath for months. The fact he is mad and has lost almost all his memory can be surmised from the opaqueness of his reddish sticky eyes. His fly is absently open, hiding gross organs in its shadow. An flaky leather bag, filled with bottles of drinking water and crinkled bags of food, opens next to him on the wooden seat. His black fingers pick the scraps from the dirty plastic bags to put into his hairy, slavering mouth. The contentment on his grimy, unshaven face looks genuine when he gives passersby a toothless smile. Everyone automatically keeps a distance from him when he speaks loudly to them as he sees fit.

This man is a nuisance! I want to go to him and shout into his crazy face. He should cover up that obscene fly! Then a golden object lighting a cigarette flashes across my mind. Suddenly, I know the deeper reason for having to shout.

Something is dreadfully wrong, today! Right in front, a frightening paradox is threatening to rend the world apart. Everything looks so fine here because the people work hard for it. Yet, the man left to rot and die, who is a nuisance, has it better than any of them. Those who look fine are really rotting away. Like Howard and his girlfriend, they're the real fools – and the real bastards of the world.

Humanity must be corrected. It must be saved! I've to do something quickly. I don't want to be a preacher sounding an alarm as it's stupid. I've an idea. I am going to do something for myself instead. I'm going to prove I am free. But what do I free myself of? I must find that out first. Then I find the object to free myself of. I'm going to prove I'm free of this world and myself, all the unresolved issues notwithstanding. I'm not harried like those fools. I already know by heart what the conditions are.

I think it's crazy, but I'm not going to change my mind. I turn round to face the human traffic, mostly surging, claws in front like frantic spiders, against me. My heart pounds loud and hard against my chest. I hesitate. I think straightaway, the hesitation is a mistake. I mustn't continue thinking! The crowd looks crazy though probably innocent, as I scan the top of their unhuman heads. My own head spins as I raise both hands and glare at the faces. But all I'm doing is try to hold those spiders back. I have to give it to them and chase them away. Frighten them! I remember Feng said: be cruel in order to be kind! I smack my open palms violently into the empty air. Repeatedly, I smack the air.

I don't speak Japanese beyond a few words. The Japanese don't speak English, but with Chinese languages, they fare even worse.

"Go back!" I find myself shouting in English. "Do you hear me?" I try to shout even louder. "You are all stupid!" I've reached my limit in loudness. I wonder if there is even one person who understands what I'm saying.

The idea hits me I don't really know why I am doing this. I try not to think about it. Passersby look at me. Their mouths drop open and they run from me. Children turn and gape at me like baby spiders with wide-open eyes. It hits me that those tortured souls now understand. What I did works!

But as quickly as it began, everyone continues their brisk pace as before – hurrying. Everything is back to normal. Deep disappointment takes hold. I let out a deep sigh. I continue to walk against the crowd, consoled I've at least done my part.

I can't believe I've done it. Two policemen walk towards me, their faces strained by the burden of decision. I leave quickly before they decide to take me. As my head fills up with loud swirling sounds, I'm thankful for the arrival of common sense.

***

At last, I have a feeling I'm free. Ahead of me, the dull brownish shape of a building with Japanese characters grows larger and green. I stride quickly towards my hotel, not looking at people. I push open the stiff glass door. The bellboy with a pale face, in light brown uniform and a porter hat on his head, scampers to hold back the door.

"Are you all right, sir? Your face's very white," he says in stop-start English when I walk in.

"I'm all right! But I forgot dinner."

"Don't walk outside! We have crew menu for you. Special prices!"

"Why can't I go out?"

"Something's very wrong – outside. *Gaijin!* Foreigner! Normally – doesn't happen. Later – OK." He curls his thumb and index finger into a circle, other digits standing bent.

I walk slowly to the old lift and press the button. It brings me to the third floor, like a depressed doddering man. I go to my room and insert my key. I push open the door and close it.

***

Is everything OK for the thing? The conditions in my mind when I was trying to free myself and now, I mean.

The purpose of what I do has to come from within and shouldn't be adulterated with other postulates. It has to be carried out, only when I feel like it. Daring is never enough. Risks and dangers must be commensurate with objectives since unnecessary excess is not heroism but plain stupidity. There can be some rationalisation and a plan or strategy (these mustn't take too long to be decided on, and only a clear mind can do it), but mental games to produce a positive attitude are grounds for disqualification. Prayers, visualisation, meditation and self-hypnosis all fall into the disqualified category. Simple autosuggestions are acceptable, but should preferably not be employed. The use of stimulants and calming agents like drugs and alcohol are cheating, whereas the unavoidable consumption of everyday foods and beverages containing a few stimulants is all right, if not intentionally taken or consumed in excess.

Most of the time, of course, some forms of cheating would've been carried out to overcome fear and other negative states of mind, but there may be other reasons. Thoughts can't be avoided, and circumstances (both outside and inside me) are constantly changing. Therefore, the faster a challenge is addressed, the better. Being unaware there is some degree of external prop (as is the case most of the time) is acceptable ignorance.

I shouldn't think too much as I'm now doing. I should leave judgment on the degree of success or failure of my endeavour to others …

Chapter 3
Standby Day

I'm trembling and cold. I should've raised the room temperature before getting into bed. I tell myself it was only a dream, and I must calm down.

I had called Howard in the middle of standby to ask permission to go out for lunch. Instead, he was crying like a baby as he told me his girlfriend was having terrible labour pains.

"There's no time to tell the crew. The Assistant Purser has gone for lunch. The ambulance is downstairs. You will become the Purser!"

"What?" I said. "I have just been promoted. I don't know anything about your work. I don't know how to delegate work positions. If there is an emergency, what am I to do?"

"Please! Please! Help me! She is dying!"

"You've to find the AP. He is next in line, not me."

"I don't care. Bye! Bye! Very sorry!" He slammed the phone down.

I ordered the crew to report for work immediately. I was in a panic. Twenty minutes later, I met them in the hotel lobby. Most of the crew members were not properly dressed. Their hair was in a mess. I scolded them for their bad appearance. They shouted back that I gave them only twenty minutes, and threatened to report the matter to the local police to get me thrown into prison. Then they demanded their work positions.

"Work positions! What do you expect? I'm only a JP, just promoted. How do I know how to give work positions?"

That was when I woke up with a start.

***

I'm no longer cold.

It's standby day. But standby hasn't even started; it begins in two hours'. I still have time to go out of the hotel for lunch, so I pick up the phone to call Feng. I hope his woman has something she wants to do without him.

"Good morning, Mr Liu," Feng says cheerily. "Come to my room for lunch? I brought Gardenia bread from home. Pork floss too. Don't waste money. Tonight, we can go to a different restaurant. Or, do you have a restaurant in mind?"

I change into my T-shirt and shorts, and walk to his room which is two doors away. It's a little cold as I drag the ill-fitting hotel slippers on the dull, carpeted corridor.

His room is brown and warm. I sit by the round table, a lean knotty figure jutting out of a rounded armchair. A little higher than my head sits a bevelled lamp shade on a thin wooden stem. Feng pulls the chain hanging within the shade and draws aside the window curtain.

"I have English tea – and coffee as well – if you like," he says as light invades the room.

I tell him, self-effacingly, I prefer English tea. He has a useful pilot case for his travels, and he snaps the latches open. He removes a small box from the bag he has opened, while I fill two cups with hot water from the cylindrical boiler on the counter just above the fridge. Taking a tea bag from the box with knotty fingers, I let it sink into the hot water. I tear a sachet of powdered creamer at one of its corners, then a sachet of sugar.

Feng walks to the brown tray by the boiler and takes a green tea bag for his cup. He carries the chair from the desk to the round table and sits opposite me. As he listens to my story about Howard and his girlfriend, he spreads margarine over a slice of bread, and sprinkles it with pork floss. He eats it.

"He is a nice purser: very understanding and patient."

I raise my bare eyebrows which are like my nondescript personality. "Can someone be good when he misleads another?"

"Why not? It is not for us to judge!"

"He's cheating her with lies. You can't see he is a bastard?"

"Everyone is born good. He has his reasons. Maybe, he has a bad childhood."

"I would agree if you say all men are alike. Each person is born neither good nor bad. To me, one is neither good nor bad. Good or bad is a perception; by themselves, they don't exist. How good or how bad one is, is due to conditioning. But one has to be wary of a bastard."

"I don't accept that. We must always be forgiving. Never judge a person. We are not qualified to do that because we don't know enough, and we don't have good judgment. Have you tried it? When someone slaps you on the right cheek, give him the left as well. I have. It works!"

"Really?"

"Once, I flew with Ramesh Nair. I tell you, that Purser is a real bastard. On board, he wanted me to do this and that. But everything I did, he criticised and wanted it his way. It was like he knew everything, and I was always wrong. After work, the same thing. In London, we went to Lee Ho Fook for lunch. He ordered everything as he liked.

"On the way from London to Bahrain, we stopped at Rome and Athens. From Athens to Bahrain, it was only four hours and full-load. After service, he demanded the crew go out with a large tray of drinks every twenty minutes, even though ninety-nine percent of passengers were asleep. The crew were already so tired as this was the third sector, and they had no time to eat.

"I suggested someone go into the cabin and ask those who were awake if they like a drink. He insisted two persons should go out, one on each side of the cabin with a large tray of juices and water. He said this looked more professional, and I was lazy. Then he called me to the First Class and talked for half an hour when I had other important duties to finish. He wanted me to apologise to him in Bahrain in front of all the JPs, because he claimed I embarrassed him in front of them."

I remember flying with Ramesh when I was a steward. "That short guy needed lots of deodorant and behaved as if the crew were slaves in the cabin. He wobbled on three-inch soles and usually stuck his jaw out like a pit bull following its master."

Feng raises his large eyes. "Anyway, you know what I did? After dinner, in a crew joint in Bahrain, we gathered in his room for a drink. There were eight of us: the senior crew and a few others. He asked me when I was going to apologise. So, I said loudly for all to hear. 'Please forgive me, my god. You are the smartest man in Cabin Crew, the one I respect most.' I then knelt before him and touched the floor with my head three times." Feng smiles triumphantly. "He didn't answer, and he dared not look at me. For the rest of the trip, he never disturbed me. Maybe, he never liked me. Maybe, I didn't follow him blindly."

I hesitate. "When I was a steward, he called my room in Dubai to ask me to buy lunch for him. He said he wasn't feeling well and the desert sun was too hot, but when I brought him the food, he looked fine. He didn't pay me for that."

Feng frowns as his voice hardens. "I remember now. After that meal at Lee Ho Fook, he asked the new hostess to pay for his meal first. He said he overspent his pounds and would return her in dollars in the hotel. He didn't pay her. She asked him for it on board, but he said he would pay later. After the flight, she could not find him."

***

I remember the frightful dream. Waking up in panic, I had immediately relived the chaotic moments. Intense feelings and immediacy helped paste that dream onto the surface of my consciousness. Had that not been the case, it would have fallen – further with each passing moment – into the abyss. Pieces and perhaps, the whole dream would become practically irrecoverable.

As I try telling Feng what happened, the dream is progressively losing clarity. Colours and sounds are fading. A dream remembered somehow stays slippery. Each time it slips, it becomes more slippery. Soon, only the skeleton remains. And from the words I mumble, hang only fleshy bits of colours and feelings.

The same is happening to my memory of Howard and his girlfriend in splendid Ginza. It's more stable than the dream, but there is no difference except a matter of degree. I'm confused now whether the incident in Ginza or the dream is the true reality. I swear by the former because I remember the feeling it was real. It also relates to my present experience better than the dream. But what logical basis is there for believing what I remembered is reality? And on what basis the present is the reality? Then that linkage to Ginza, provided by memory, becomes tenuous, and each event becomes as blur and unreal as the other …

I try to see some certainty in what I've described about Howard in Ginza. That causes my memory to slip further.

"You shouldn't let Ramesh have a free lunch. If I were you …"

I realise with a jolt that Feng is still sitting there in his pyjamas – speaking. He is talking about Ramesh. But am I dreaming? Did he return to the subject or has he been talking about it?

Feng expects me to say more about Ramesh. I've to fish the incident from cloudy waters. Nothing, besides what I already said! Then bits and pieces float up like jetsam. When I fail to hold the information, they slip and sink again. Regret now clings to my mind, like sticky rice to my teeth, distracting me, clouding the waters further. I know the pieces are there, but I can't see them, nor hear, nor smell them.

As I think, I use words without conviction.

Then suddenly, words roll out like a printed sheet from a printer. They feel meaningless, but I mustn't do anything which stops them coming. I "know" those eloquent words represent the truth. I "know" it because anyone talking like me would.

"It was one of my first flights in the Jumbo. He did nothing except coming to my galley now and then, 'talking cock' to girls. Everyone asked what he liked to eat or drink, as they were afraid of him. This guy picked on one or two persons. It was smart as he couldn't handle more people on a trip. No one wanted to be his victim."

The words stop coming. The sheet is stuck. I've been thinking. I was hoping the right stuff would appear. I was worried the right stuff wasn't coming. I know I have to stop thinking, and let go.

The words come flooding back. "At the preflight briefing, he warned us not to take anything from the aircraft. But it was okay to take for own consumption. Later, I realised that before the aircraft arrived in a city, he would ask someone to carry alcohol for him.

"I went to the First Class to study the galleys as he said I had to do that. That was when I caught him red-handed. He was stealing those First Class gold-plated figurines meant for passengers."

Feng helps himself to another piece of the soft bread. He walks to the boiler to make coffee.

"Do you like more tea? Was the load full?"

"I'll help myself." I take two slices of bread, spread them with margarine, then the pork floss – and make another tea. I put the two slices together, the sides with floss facing each other. "The load wasn't full, so there were extra figurines. He pushed them quickly into his bag and pretended nothing happened. I wanted no trouble and walked away."

I gobble the bread, feeling the lumps crawl down my throat.

"You did the right thing. It's not your business. Sometimes, you have to walk away. The airline is rich." Feng's wide mouth looks generous. His eyes appear knowing.

I vouch he rarely filches from the aircraft. When he did, it was always something small he really needed. I drink my tea with the bag still in the cup, the tag dangling out. Words keep flowing.

"Later, into Dubai, Ramesh entered my galley and passed me a bottle of Veuve Clicquot. 'Take this for me!' he said. I thought quickly. What if the customs asked where was the bottle from? Besides, I wasn't sure if the Muslim country allows a crew member to bring in alcohol. I said, 'I bought a bottle in London for my friend in Dubai.'

"Without a word, he left the galley, the bottle scrapping the floor from his hand. I understand he gave it to another steward to carry. A hostess refused to carry a bottle for him and didn't give any reason. She got troubles in Dubai. He tried getting into her room many times when he was drunk. And phoning her every half hour. That was when he called me to say he was sick and needed someone to buy lunch. …"

Feng looks at me curiously. I think he can see the lights fading in my eyes. His figure is still there, but blurry. I'm thinking. I jerk myself back to reality.

The words wouldn't come out anymore. It's hard for me to talk. Feng speaks again. I let him.

"Girls like Howard!" He has changed subject. Something about me causes it. It felt like a jerk in my head.

"Is it?"

"Girls can't resist something in him. The other day, I worked in First Class. Connie Koh, the senior hostess: she is the very beautiful and sexy one. She changed her flight to come on this one. He was asking her who she changed the flight with, how much money she gave and so on. Connie said whatever the amount, it was worth it. She told him not to worry and that she could afford it. Connie really took care of him, fixed his meal, asked him what drinks he liked all the time. She didn't forget others. She also asked the AP and the rest. Credit goes to Howard for not spoiling her. He didn't practise favouritism. He was fair to all.

"The JP in Value fancies him too. She came to First Class many times. When she saw him, she looked sad. I believed she knew Connie changed flight. Connie is much prettier than her. Did you notice something from Haneda Airport to the bus? Connie was walking with Howard, while the poor JP followed behind."

It's getting difficult to follow what Feng says. I want to think, but I can't do it in front of him. I've high regards for him, and he's talking. So I continue to listen to a story I lost interest in.

"I didn't notice this was happening. But why do bastards get beautiful girls?" I say anything which came to mind. I was desperate for something to say.

"He is handsome and nice. He has position. He is a Purser. More important: he is so soft-hearted he is vulnerable and needs protection. It is the whole deal. Women cannot resist this."

"Did you say he is vulnerable?"

"Yes!"

"What?"

"Yes!"

"How?"

"He doesn't scold the crew: even the new steward. He doesn't treat girls better than guys. Always soft spoken and uses 'please'. I heard he lend some colleagues money and never get it back. He helps anyone who asks for it. It is hard to reject a request. He gambles but not heavily."

I have to return to my room. Feng doesn't ask why when I tell him that. I stand up and walk to the brown door.

***

Feng's door closes with a thump.

Quickly, I walk to my room and forcibly insert the key. I step inside, close the door, then chain it. Slapping my forehead with my palm, I say angrily: "I want Feng to solve my problem, but prefer a simple solution: a mother of all solutions, perhaps a panacea. And all we did was gossip ..."

True: whatever we talked about could be relevant to my problems, and I saw that from the beginning, yet this is only possible. I might as well say nothing is unrelated. I had wanted to get on track by lobbing direct questions at Feng, yet I didn't do that. This was what I had worried would happen.

I could start all over by returning to Feng's room, right now. The fact is the longer I wait, the more chances are for me to lose focus and forget what I have to say.

Despair! I don't understand why the next thing I do is walk into the toilet. I look at myself in the mirrors. I flinch, but I am unstoppably drawn to the familiar images. They're there all right, but it's impossible to describe the feeling. It's like I can't believe it. I can't believe something could exist. I can't see why they have to exist in that manner and why they look like that. I daren't touch my face. Something would happen to the images if I do.

I think: *these objects appear to be me*: *I must have been good looking. I should preserve every image at each moment.*

I've lost my freedom: this time, to solve one problem because another is thrust upon me. Both are important and need immediate attention. Both are the same problems, the old problems. Only I can give them that attention. Only I'm willing.

I look at my face again. I'm not sure whether to praise it or to praise myself.

I can't bear it anymore, and try not to think about it. I can't! I stare at the image desperately to induce acceptance. I'm about to accept it – maybe I did …

Musical chairs: that's what these problems are, and the music is a dirge.

I rush out of the toilet, put on warm clothes and wrap my overcoat over my numb body. I pull on my shoes with shaking hands. I don't bother to comb my hair. Once I pull the door shut, I rush to the lift and enter it. What am I doing? Get away because I can't take it anymore. I've fallen into dirty water, but I won't allow myself to sink further. I try to get up. My heart is dead. I have to sort out my problems with care and urgency. I'm angry, yet I shouldn't blame myself? No one, nothing should be blamed. I'm absolutely dejected. Anger took over the despair.

The lift opens and I rush out. Standby has started, but I don't care.

***

I walk, my heart entangled in an uncomfortable knot, frail shoulders heavy with unseen burden. I try to hold on to something, but there's nothing. I walk faster. A power surges inside me. Driven by anger and dejection, it lifts me. Thigh muscles move my legs forward with powerful strides.

I look at the sea of faces around me. They all look hungry for something to change their lives; yet for most of them, there is a veneer of satisfaction and smugness. They remind me of irritating passengers on my flights. If I were serving them now, I wouldn't entertain unreasonable demands. I will do what I want. I will think if I want to, because freedom is mine.

Like the last time, someone shouted at me when he couldn't get his choice of meal as it had run out. I told him, "You paid for getting from point A to B in safety and comfort. Let me remind you it's a tiny fraction of the total cost." He looked at me, completely subdued. He didn't talk to my superior, and he didn't write in. I believe I had put some perspective into his head.

Objects, smells, and sounds swirl past me. Pleasant or unpleasant, it makes no difference. On my right is a huge space leading to something imposing. People walk towards it, getting sucked in. Wooden signs are nailed to the trees. English words on one signpost say, "Imperial Palace Ahead".

I educated myself by reading a lot. Those words ring loudly in my ears. When Feng uttered them that night, I was immediately reminded of my similar inclination. In my case, I already tell myself to learn everything, to think about anything. No angle should be missed, no stone unturned. Every hole has to be patched up, so that understanding and perceptions could be perfect.

The fact I can't remember Feng answered my question that night, disturbs me. He said everything worth doing was only for humans, and I had asked if other beings matter – whether he cared for animals and plants at all – but I couldn't keep him focused on the subject. Soon, we were talking about something else, and I found it beyond my ability to bring the subject back. He's not the only person I had this problem with. He didn't give me the impression he escaped on purpose, but I can't forget a hole remains in his philosophy.

Then this morning, he said Ramesh slapped him on the right and he gave his left, and it worked. But I can't see how his antics of kneeling before the egoistic man were forgiving. On the contrary, I felt he was sarcastic, and it was pugnacity that worked. I wanted to discuss it with him after he told me about this, but a moment of politeness and the wish for normalcy drew me back. After that, my will petered out and continued to weaken each moment the meeting proceeded further. It seems the nagging pain for failing to make Feng relook his humanitarian philosophy that night caused the weakness this morning.

The truth is I don't get blindly influenced by anyone or anything. I went through the stages of perception on my own because I exist in a world of my own. When someone tried to teach me something, it hardly entered my head because I paid scant attention to it. In fact, I couldn't pay attention to it. If a little of what I heard, saw or read were to inspire me, it would be sieved by the relentless scrutiny of my being. It would be wrung dry till the tortured self couldn't continue to spin. Nothing, as far as I remember, came out unchanged.

The Palace is pregnant with Japanese culture and history. Culture and history are what I am always interested in. There are clues leading to the understanding of mankind and Truth – and other subareas of knowledge (like science), too. But it would be too much for me today.

If I continue walking, I'll definitely get to Ginza. It has much to offer too. I already know something about Ginza, but there is more to be learnt. I should make my knowledge of Ginza more complete. I won't get lost in the Ginza, but I can't say that of the Palace whose vast grounds threaten to swallow me up and confuse. The Ginza lies on a broad straight road. The Japanese characters for it are simple enough to remember, and there are some English words too.

I stop as I'm getting further from the Palace, but nearer the Ginza. The decision which route to take has to be made based on the present, not the future or the past. It has already shifted from the original position, and is getting worse with each step I make. I don't want to let the convenience of being near the Ginza make me want to go there and influence my decision. Each direction has its own merits and consequences, but one is better or worse. One is the truth. One is truthful to me. Only one can be taken.

If I go to Ginza, I'll try not to stray too far from the main road or I would get lost. I try hard to avoid other considerations, as it has been tough enough.

It's more than difficult to decide.

In anger, I lurch forward.

***

I don't feel lonely, though I'm alone. Everything is mine, but nothing belongs to me. They are beautiful and ugly at the same time.

I should appreciate the glamorous buildings and things. Yet my awareness of the beauty stays at the edge of my being, submerged under the power consuming me. I am immune to mental pain. At present, I'm not afraid of physical pain. I feel shielded with invisible armour. I'm invulnerable.

At this junction, the road is clear but people are waiting for a tiny man to turn green. I've no patience with rules and regulations today. I cross the road and leave behind sheepish faces envying me. A car comes. Evasive eyes see me. I take my time to cross the road naturally.

***

On the right is a wide street where ubiquitous rectangles of different colours are perched on the face of low buildings. Below these unlit neon signs is a line of flashy cars. The area is buzzing with activity. Men in smart dark suits get in and out of ponderous Cadillacs and Lincolns. Attractively dressed females walk quickly. Some women are wrapped snugly in colourful, sparkling clean kimonos. Their feet, covered with white socks, shuffle quickly as they take dainty quaint steps in slippers.

I smell excitement. I'm in the company of the *yakuza* and the geishas. I walk towards them. I want to see and learn about them and one day, I shall write about them. They're dangerous if I don't keep my distance, but people living dangerously are usually in touch with some hard truths.

I stand there and consciously immerse myself in this niche of the underworld. I walk closer for a stronger feel. Shifty eyes follow movements. My eyes too as I examine everything within sight. My hands, hidden in the sides of my overcoat, feel they hold some deadly weapons. An object with an passionless face. I'm sure I look professional. A dangerous hoodlum or a brave detective? Doesn't matter!

Now I see the women's red and pink faces, clearly. The thickly powdered objects are like colourful make-up worn by artistes in Chinese operas. The eyes, heavily lined black and maroon, focus on me and look away.

Pinstripes stand out on the men's suits. Craggy faces are deeply lined and natural. Their eyes are hard like stones. Breaths smell burnt. Cigarettes light up, and smoke twirls about.

Danger sustains my freedom, keeping out the thing.

A hidden door in front of the building opens, and a man walks out. There is a dirty look on his handsome face. He comes near and opens a hand. A horrible stump on the last joint of his little finger displaces the distal phalanx. The bone had been chopped off as a punishment from his crime boss for some mistake he must now regret. He stares at me, then shouts in a gruffly voice towards a black car across the street. I'm sure I'm not his quarry, only when the car doors open.

Two burly, middle-aged men with rogue faces emerge while the driver stays behind the wheel. They approach the man near me, their colourful tattoos peeking from uncovered hands. A knife flashes from the hand with the stump – and both men dash to the car. Next moment, they return with rods in their hands. They charge at their lone enemy and hit him with the rusty green pipes – but as the man falls, he manages an arc with his long knife.

A howl cuts the air as red bright spatters appear in progression on the clean tarmac. The wounded man staggers to the car as his accomplice hits the fallen man with his iron pipe again and again. Blood squirts in various directions! The knife, lined red on one side, clatters gently near my feet.

The street fell silent. Suddenly, shouts come from everywhere, as men in black appear. The assailant flings the pipe at the body on the floor, notices it miss and sprints to the car. Once he enters it, the door slams shut. Three tensed faces at the windows, stare ahead. Then, the car rushes off – honking and screeching – and the crowd opens up instantly to give way.

As swiftly as it started, some of the men carry their comrade through the indistinctive door. Two or three tough men shout and wave the groups away. I melt into the crowd, scattering like frightened ants into the chaotic void.

Released from troubled existences, the faces of relief mirror mine. The power of adventure providing economical and clear moments like this, for the masses, will last a little longer at least. The crowd turns into parochial individuals, returning to old ways. Soon, they will be overwhelmed again by their own separate worlds.

The thing is waiting. I don't want it to stay away for long, anyway. It will soon find me, anyway.

Chapter 4

First Day at Downtown Los Angeles

After I got away from the gang fight at the Ginza, I walked slowly back to the hotel, feeling with each step, the sense of power gradually leaving. Inside my room, I learnt there was no standby call-up and was immensely relieved. The next day, we left Tokyo on a short flight for Los Angeles.

The weather is nice in LA. It's cool in the afternoon when we approach the large downtown hotel. On the bus, Feng says he feels we are entering a fortress in a totally deserted area. Once darkness descends, and during weekends and public holidays, beggars and miscreants are the only people on the streets.

Within the hotel; restaurants, small shops, salons and even a clinic provide all sorts of goods and services so long as one agrees to part with money. Inside my room, I wear a sweater over my shirt and take the transparent lift down to the third storey.

At a corner of the brightly lit CJ Restaurant, I sit – inside the object only I know too well – hoping no crew member would walk in or see it. I'm thankful everyone seems to have their own programmes. I've a three-day layover without standby, and tomorrow is a full day off. Feng didn't ask me for a meeting, and I didn't want to ask him.

The object has an all-round cover which blocks out unwelcome stuff. Two small slits at the top with transparent shields let in orange lights which sneaked through reddish lampshades. Behind the openings, a slimy mass always in touch with all other parts of the object, tells me the throbbing centre is emotionally numbed. Channeled by funnels at both sides, waves crash through tunnels and get decoded with the help of sensitive drums.

The slimy mass deduces big Americans are talking loudly in English, using strange words with interesting intonations. It also concludes those living objects are mostly blacks and whites. The blacks wear over-sized clothes with jeans almost falling off their buttocks. In the background is the ever-sawing movement of jazz music.

Movements make things and events. Fleshy tongs put fries on the surface of an eager muscle. It's hard to control the shredder breaking the tasty hamburger with gusto. Potent seepage softens the foreign matter within the enclosure.

Caffeine in the tea enters streams to reach the throbbing centre. It spurs the organ and the tired mind.

On the other side of the massive globe, infinitesimally transient points start moving. The points are as insignificant as each other, but very important to themselves and their friends and enemies. They stir and get off their beds. They make elaborate rituals only themselves and a few notice and understand: like flies rubbing their forelegs against each other on a breakfast table. People look forward to the new day or dread it. Those leaving for work but woke up late, will panic, take control or be insouciant about it.

If I dropped some coins into a so-called machine at the lobby, I should hear voices. They'll probably tell me what they are doing or going through. But I don't want to lose pieces of metal I've collected since I will meet my mother and sisters eventually anyway. They're certainly preparing breakfast for themselves which they will soon eat. An object which appeared before this one, is perched astride a narrow seat on a tangle of hard substance. Its buttocks are calloused and numbed from years of sitting. Its eyes are watching, its hands in firm control. The feet rotate fast and slow, slow and fast as it brings passengers safely to their destinations. Powerful muscles push the pedals dutifully, only to relax. Lungs contract to expand. Air rushes in and out of the body as the pedals pull a chain. The chain turns a wheel forcing along two other wheels. The three wheels go round and round, and the vehicle bumps now and then; turns here and there. The tarmac races backwards like a rushing river.

Yet, this massive globe is another transient point in the limitless universe.

***

This insignificant object is tired and needs a nap. It's still tuned to a faraway place, where day just began. It was working all night, but it's still awake. It can't forget, and its mind is moving beyond.

I'm staring blankly through the glass wall at the empty corridor. It's not bright there, but I see clearly what goes on. The doors to my right open to reveal a black man in tight jeans and a rumpled blazer. He stands inside the lift, with his eyes glued to the floor. He steps onto the corridor, a dirty hat pressed snugly on his head.

There is a dance forward as his body bobs on thin springy legs. His wide turgid lips open and shut. A long tongue sneaks in and out. His jet-black face turns from side to side, and sees mine looking at it from a table. He sticks the tongue out more. It stays briefly. It's pink too. The face is totally crazed and spaced out. The eyes – wide open – look down a twitching broad nose.

I must have caused the next event for without turning, he bounces back to the lift and turns around. His back always to the front, he walks and bounces back and forth along the corridor. Sometimes, he looks left and right slightly, and at the floor for orientation. He has done this often it's easy for him. The notion of the hotel being a fortress collapses straightaway.

The black is outside the restaurant. Through the transparent wall, I see and know what is happening from inside. People talk and sip coffee inside. At the counter, a fat Negress collects pieces of paper and metal with capricious values (above their worth mostly) in return for stuff she gives. A man carries the items on a tray to a table. He's going to eat and drink in this space we call a restaurant.

Outside, the black peers into the restaurant and sees objects get up to leave. Things and events exist outside the body I'm in. Tiny objects within it stay open to work with it. The soft mass called the brain, tells me what it perceives through these organs. I feel with the heart, smell with my nose and touch with my skin. I hear through tunnels called ears and see with openings called eyes. My eyes mostly see in front of the main object or the body. To see the sides and the back, I twist my neck and turn my head. I can also turn the body.

The brain and the mind exist together. The mind exists with the body, and works through the brain. The brain manages the body. I'm mind and body. I'm the result of interactions, mainly, between my mind and my body. Without the body, there is no mind. Without the mind, there is no body. I don't know the mind exists first, or the body. I can't say one is more important than the other.

I don't exist. I am not something, but I'm also not nothing. The "world" is there.

Something happening outside me happens within too. One event! Objects outside me are still active. But some have slowed and need to rest.

**

An internal event stimulates me when it tries to meet a condition in me. A thought arises, and I realise liquid has filled up my bladder. If I don't do something, the body and the clothes covering it will get wet. The brain messages the heart and other parts of the body. All this occurs in me. Thoughts change all the time. The mind thinks it can control the bladder, and there is no urgency. It tells the brain to wait a little.

I look down at the tray in front of me. Fragments lying there are safe from me. Half a fry shrivels on the tray mat. A crumb or two of hamburger bread hide in the shadows of crumpled wrappers. The paper cup is empty. Brown rings inside, at the top and centre, prove it was once quite full.

Something on the tray mat catches my eye, and my hand pushes the mess to one side. In black and white, a lone Negro wearing a jacket is laughing. The young man is walking on the uneven cobbled street alongside uninteresting warehouses and sacks of cargoes. Two horses stand in front of a covered wagon, full of goods, at the end of the street.

I think of the black man outside this orangey place. I look up. His back is resting on the balustrade, and he is staring at me. He and the negro on the tray seem to be the same person. He was laughing all by himself on the cobbled street some time ago, and then he appeared when the lift doors opened. Now, he is alone in front of me, beyond the glass, and he has noticed me.

The wagon in the photograph is ancient and the caption says: *The City of Angels, 1898*. It's logical the Negro in the picture is dead. He came into existence a hundred years ago, but now he's gone. Somewhere in the US, he was walking and laughing, and someone took a picture of him, and he probably didn't even know it. Something entered his mind which made him laugh so heartily.

I wonder those were thoughts about himself or others. Were they kind or mean? I don't care how he lived, but he grew old and then died. Or, did he die young, not long after this photo was taken? More than eighty years after that enigmatic walk, during which he laughed to himself; more than eighty years after that photo was taken, he still exists, as young as he was. Of course, it was on paper, but at least he exists. He will exist as long as this picture exists.

Of all the points, another man took on the role of a photographer and chose this point of a Negro, of all the moments and locations, for his picture. The Negro was one of the few lucky people who had thousands of copies of themselves made this way. Actually, it's millions in his case, and he didn't even have to make them. If this copy is destroyed, there would be millions left. And after all these copies, the original is lying somewhere. Finally, there is the negative which can be used to make more copies.

No wonder people are dissatisfied with wealth since the more one has, the more one wants. The more secure a person feels, the more he or she needs, to feel secure.

***

These are vicious traps.

When the black man still outside the restaurant, stepped onto the corridor, his face was totally bewildered. That and his walking backwards were moments I wish to record, with or without his permission. I want to capture those moments on paper – though that only takes care of the picture. Then if I want to, I can place the pictures next to the Negro on the cobblestone street. When someone sees the three photos side by side, he or she can imagine what happened by the warehouses, somewhere in existence about eighty years ago, and all that happened up to this moment.

A photo is evidence which can't be altered. (It would be more accurate in colour than in black and white.) Any attempt to doctor it can always be proved. Technology already makes it easy to capture sounds at the same time as pictures. Smells, taste and feelings, in no particular order, could eventually be captured too. For now though, I'm content with a picture. I know straightaway it's related to a person or an event when I see it, which isn't the case when I listen to recorded sounds. (How can one be sure the sounds are connected to something? A person has to rely on witnesses or experts for that.)

While a photo is a possession and isn't part of a man, the body is a part of him. Both objects represent the man, though the photograph is mainly a record of the body.

The inanimate photo is also different from the body in that the organic world changes fast. It breaks down slower than a body (which grows and deteriorates quickly), but any damage is far worse since a picture is usually less extensive than a body. A damaged picture can't repair itself, unlike a body.

Technology makes life more efficient, but there are two sides to everything. It's now very easy to store information, as it is to lose it. The gap should become more pronounced in future as efficiency continues to improve. It'll become easier for something to happen. When you lose something, you lose more. A slip already results in immense loss or destruction. Wilful destruction is now easily carried out. If this problem isn't addressed, the responsibility of a person will become heavier and heavier. I don't see how this could be solved. It contradicts what people expect of technology. A person's frail shoulders are destined to carry an ever heavier burden till he or she drops dead.

Modern products are constantly changing and need regular maintenance. Time and effort are needed to understand and record procedures. Updating complicated skills is a continuous process as the relentless competition between the forces of destruction and protection stretch into infinity.

Sometimes, so many pictures are taken one can't count them, and still the person goes on snapping. It's like two mirrors reflecting each other. If you were to see the last image, you would find there are more images than you think, and you have not seen the last. And when you see that new last, the same thing would happen, and you would believe again the final end is within reach.

It's too late to capture that moment on paper. All I wanted was for an event to record it, but unfortunately the event didn't materialise. I didn't bring along a camera because I thought it was a burden. I can't say the failure has nothing to do with me because I could have done better. It's hard to excuse myself when I knew I had to bring the camera from the beginning. The occasion for the event is past and doesn't exist anymore.

I can regret all I "want", but the opportunity will never return. I feel closer to the loss through regret (as though I'm getting it back), yet the gulf is widening every moment. Regret is a useless attempt to reverse time. I know I can't go back from the start, but I keep trying. Then why is regret part of me? Why is it so seductive and powerful? Why the pain sweet? The more I regret, the larger the issue becomes as it gathers more baggage, and then the more I owe regret.

Perhaps, regret survives evolution so one could see mistakes and improve. That's possible only if I stop regretting. But like all tendencies, it goes on turning like a tape on a recorder. Once the tape has run its course, it's a matter of time before it gets replayed. I'm lucky if I forget to continue to regret. Does the tape have to break before regret stops?

How wonderful it is, if there is no regret! Then I would want sadness removed. There should only be good feelings. Eradicate pain and sickness. Ask for eternal life in heaven. In that case, I shouldn't live. I still hope what is bad is actually good; or at the end, it's good or at least neutral. I'll know when I see it.

Perhaps someday, I can't look back as there are only the present and the future. I will look forwards and outwards. If only everything is this or that, and there are no grey areas. Then, I believe something or I don't, and I do something or I don't. When there are no dilemmas, a coin has just one side.

When one finds out there was nothing to regret about, one could regret regretting. This sort of cycles goes on and on. There is no good or bad in anything when everything is considered, any more than you can't change anything from what is. When one has this insight, ambition will be a meaningless emotion. It'll fall to the ground like a discarded robe, and only basic motivations like survival will be left.

Good or bad is meaningless by itself. The mind confuses … . Someday, there would be no world. Somewhere, perhaps …

Even if I have a camera with me, I don't think I will use it. I won't want taking pictures to distort an experience. I want a complete experience, and that's the contradiction. The more I try to have a pure experience, the more frustrated I am.

Each moment is recorded and archived by default. Nothing has to be done. An image is stored permanently. The past is anchored to the present. I should let history look after itself. There is infinite storage space for anything in a dot and beyond it.

But one cannot be sure who and what the person in a photo is, just as I'm not sure my body is mine.

Perhaps, no one will see the truth. I should let it be. By saying that, I'm not letting it be. Not letting go and letting go are natural since both tendencies are from man who is part of nature. That feels unnatural. Give up thinking! Do it! Just give up! Suspended, I can't move. I don't know what to do. I feel the rope round my neck. I'm standing on tip-toe, hands tied, as thoughts push me to and fro.

A whitish form appears in my forehead and breaks into ideas about the photographer. I can assume whatever is standing in the void is the person. He or she sees the Negro from a distance. On the spur of the moment, he or she makes that decision. The person shifts the box hanging from the neck, from one side of his body to the front, and snaps it open. He looks down at the square screen, sees laughter on the black face and adjusts the position of the picture. He notes the presence of the horses standing without choice and buildings which couldn't bother. He thinks the picture is good enough, that he can't risk waiting another moment.

Then, the heart beating fast, the person presses that button.

It's possible it didn't happen this way. But the photo adorns millions of trays. The person who took this has some sort of quality. If the press likes, they can call it "genius". Talent, quick thinking or plain luck? It doesn't matter which, but he was responsible for the existence of this picture. The person was gone, but his legacy continues. The legacy isn't part of him, but it represents him.

Only the Negro exists on the tray mat and is remembered. The Negro is immortalised! It isn't right nobody even thinks there was someone else out there, walking on the street. This person made the picture, but no one cares to know who he or she is except me. How would the photographer feel if he realises this? But to have one person think of him is enough. It's as good as the whole world thinking of him. It proves he exists.

Yet, he or she shouldn't care what people feel. Like dreaming about a dream, feelings are a dream in a dream. Existence or inexistence: what effect has these wrangling thoughts brought them? Is there any difference made that matters?

***

The creak of a closing door! Sound waves have entered the tunnels and hit the drums. My brain concludes the black has entered the restaurant. In the bright light, he looks small and wizened. He's nearly as short as Ramesh – like a small Asian – whereas I'm used to seeing big African Americans.

He looks older than I thought, and there is no hair on his head.

His inverted hat held out, he walks and pushes the object at me. I drop a note into the round shadow. His bloodshot eyes are still spaced out and he doesn't thank me. The dark lips are clamped shut, as he walks to the seat near the counter. The plump Latino remains deep in thought. His head shakes left and right, and the black walks to the remaining customer on my left, across the aisle.

I recall a black lady limp through the door not long ago. She is facing me diagonally, reading a religious magazine at her table. Her opaque eyelids dangle, as her hand moves uncertainly to open the purse in her handbag. She licks the tip of the forefinger. The moistened finger and a thumb feel a note in the purse and unfold it carefully. They lift it to the face and drop it into the imploring hat.

The black man disappears from my view.

"What do you like?" A girl's sulky voice comes from the counter behind me.

"Do you've a light?" It's his whiny voice.

"We don't serve lights."

"I only want a light."

"I said, 'No lights!' No smoking in this space."

A pair of thick-framed spectacles tugs the black lady's large head, and rest on the concave bridge to a shiny knob. Black bushy hair looks like a loose wig. The lamp above her ball face illuminates mysterious features but doesn't accentuate them.

Her face is an archive. Every line or crease tells a story. She went through a troubled life. As a young woman, she was beautiful and brimming with confidence. But now middle-aged and normal, she looks at society with overflowing suspicion. If her old flame loved her for her beauty, she could have realised passion – like every phenomenon – is transient and dependent.

The black man appears. Without permission, he lowers his small bottom and adjusts his flat body between my table and the opposite seat. (He is attracted to this miserly blob of companionship.)

The ball turns. The "wig" bows. Her eyes stare above her glasses at the thin eccentric face. The old man doesn't bat an eyelid despite the obvious effort.

"Where are you from?" He asks me instead, with concern.

I don't want to talk, but he has no baggage and no dignity. I can be frank, and there would be no waste of time and energy.

"I'm from nowhere. I leave later." I don't look at him, like he didn't look at the woman.

His ashy face is expressionless. He realises I wasn't funny. "I stay as long as I can because they'll kick me out anyway. Then I go to the park, sit on a bench; or if it's raining, get into shops and malls. I dress well – or I can't enter." He continues, "I also go to the Grey Dog Bus Terminal, but I can't stay long. It's filthy and smelly with crazies." A small finger screws a small head. "This place is nice. Good people like you and the loony behind you. Not she! She's too sane."

Luckily, she's in a world of her own.

It's easy to want to support this man. We're lost people with complementary qualities. He's eloquent whereas I think so much I shake sometimes, when I speak. I aspire to be like him. With practically no possessions and place in society, he is free. But I can't be like him. I'm always trying to clear my doubts. I need to be careful though. I've not come across someone or something I liked or supported which hadn't eventually betrayed me. Rich or poor, powerful or lowly, haughty or humble: they are the same. Everyone and everything turned out to be blemished enough for me to want to discard them.

"I only got two dollars from you and her."

The lady is nodding. Dissatisfaction distorts her semiconscious face. Something is hurting.

"Typical! She thinks I disgrace her race, yet we are the same people. She gave a dollar, but … ?" He turns up his nose.

She's frowning. Between two gentle puffs, her mouth becomes a pointed knot. She could be scolding her ex-lover as two nebulous drawstrings pull away from a full pouch to the sides.

Choosing a metaphor for the battered object with minute movements is a heavy responsibility since it will become part of my memory. I become drowsy when I can't decide, but I am not giving up. I'm nodding – and the black too.

Spidery threads fall from the open mouth as droopy papayas heave. Balls roll stealthily behind eyelids shut. Nostrils expand and contract. Air wheezes in and out laboriously.

A longish speck struggles on the smudgy blazer opposite, gripping a white dot. Its legs cling desperately to the fabric – right of the breast pocket. Two broken wings glisten on the lapel. A lost flying ant in pain brought food along. Has it left its group for freedom, and its frantic feelers are searching for shelter? It almost fell again many times. Its abdomen feels a niche in the pocket lining and pushes backwards. A protrusion with two minuscule eyes juts out and dangles in the air. Tired jaws struggle not to drop the morsel into the abyss as forelegs grope helplessly.

Three nodding objects, drawn to each other, each preserving its self while outside, the music keeps churning. I'm extremely drained. I can't sleep properly. I have a room upstairs, and I'm going there to rest horizontally.

I hope to wake up refreshed. Each time I wake, I'm overall lesser compared to previous cycles. Jet lag, insomnia, radiation – and beyond control, ever-present time will have exacted their toll. Rests and activities alternate in cycles and then permanence. If there is such a state as permanent rest!

I shan't see the dreamers anymore! Bluff and burn yourselves away!

***

Dawn creeps at six, into another part of the world across the Atlantic. A new day is beginning in a heated restaurant I patronised each time I walked through the market. Vigilant heads peek out of a small crack near the edge of a table. The tiny objects snoop on the surface, feelers twirling in the cigarette smoke. Soon, tentative lines form behind temporary leaders. The lines break up as more and more ants leave to join a lengthening column. The line surges forward to their new-found objective.

They reemerge with prizes held in front by determined jaws. They don't eat the food but carry them home stoically. The returning ants and their proceeding comrades stop to hug each other if they aren't carrying something – before they hurry on.

A circle turns, advancing slowly, as the ants heave a huge burden which wobbles. Later, they would happily stow it in the gap they came from. They would stack and arrange it in a cave: caves which are little more than tiny holes to customers arriving for breakfast at the coffee shop in wintry Amsterdam.

"These damned ants," says the burly object with a heavy Dutch accent as it lowers its six-foot-five frame carefully onto the wobbly chair. "Each morning, they arrive on a table before me. When I sleep at night, they crawl into my helpless mind."

The mind decides, and the brain acts. The big hand coming from the huge object, takes the small box sitting on one side of the ashtray. The other big hand takes a stick from the box. One end of the stick scratches the rough side of the box.

The short lean man, also in bricklayer overalls, bends towards the flame, a cigarette dangling from his mouth. The burly man presses the head of his cigarette against the lighted end of his friend's. He holds the lighted head towards the ants with the burden. The circle wavers and tries to detour. One or two ants release their hold in panic, and one side of the burden falls onto the table.

"Leave them alone!" the friend says in time. "They're hardworking insects, that's all. They're like the crew from the airline we flew with last month. Can you remember? Those people never stopped working to make us happy."

"You're right! I was bored," the rough voice striding out of the huge neck, says. The strayed ants return to help carry the carcass. "Anyway, that guy we met last time at this table: he is from the same airline. He is a deep guy. He looked very lost. He always missed home when away. But he also said whenever he was home, he would think of where he flew back from. Everywhere is home, but everywhere, he has no home since he is still searching."

His cigarette-smelling finger nudges a stray back. It's about to join the line when it turns to look at the gigantic protuberance. The tiny mind and the minuscule brain direct the small body. The object rises on hind legs and waves its faint feelers.

"You're grateful," the big Dutchman continues, staring at the ant. "I see. You take on any obstacle, and adapt like the crew. Society rewards you, but before you realise it, it has given your privileges to others who should work harder. You can't beat nature's system."

The short man doesn't have a loud voice. "Who're you talking to?"

"Both of you! I remember the flight. It was our first time to the Far East. That Purser who was very friendly, whose name was Eric ... He didn't do anything while the rest of the crew worked so hard. The only times I saw him, he was talking and eating. The crew would be speaking animatedly in some language, amongst themselves, but the moment he appeared, they switched immediately to English for him."

The softer voice speaks clearly. "Yes, I noticed this too. Those people worked differently from us though Liu Xiang wasn't like them. The world is unfair! But that was how they made our flight unforgettable. I cannot forget the crew. It's like when the guy was here, he seemed to be constantly peering into his mind … .

"The cabin crew were mere existents like us, though they were nice to us. I remember I told a girl it was my birthday. There were no birthday cards on board, so she and another girl made one out of a menu card and even got the Captain and the crew to sign it. At the right moment, they gathered around us and sang a happy birthday song. The lights were turned off (only a few reading lights were left on). The passengers clapped, and we drank sparkling wine at thirty thousand feet in the air. Till today, it is alive, like a movie in me, complete with colours and sounds. The actors and actresses in it never get old, and they will be there as long as I am alive."

The loud voice rumbles. "The drinks kept coming, carried by the pretty, exotic hostesses with gentle smiles. The chatter and laughter, the orange lighting, while outside was complete darkness. Those faces were haunting in the night. There were also the gentle vibrations of powerful engines, like giant cats purring in the sky. They will live forever in my mind like clinging parasites. It is painful and delightful, now it's in the past."

"Shouldn't we just drop those things?" the smaller man asks.

"Yes! It would lighten us, he said, since they use up energy. Do you remember? His father worked very hard. His mother looked after the home, and washed clothes for friends and neighbours to help out with expenses when the children were young. She suddenly died of cancer, and the unfortunate man was totally unprepared. He knew death is inevitable, but he could never feel the urgency his close ones were also affected just because he knew. He had important problems to sort out first. Even when she was alive, he would feel excused because that was his greater duty. He tried dropping what he was trying hard to understand for a long time, but found himself only perpetuating it in other ways. That part of his life with the characters: he carries forever. (He said he never weighed it with a machine.) He wished someone would carry his story in turn, since he is doing his part, but the sensitive soul also hoped not. It is a burden for the person, even if the story is beautiful."

"What happens near the equator, is happening here. He thought it is wasteful. All the joy and pain; at the end, for nothing! It's afternoon there. Soon, people will finish work and go home to the warmth of family and friends, though not in his case.

"He said we are some of the active parts of nature's storage of information. The part which was him was too active. The body and the face are facilities. He was very unhappy they are temporary.

"The city he was going to: it's neither morning nor night now. Any time and place, he is probably thinking or dreaming."

Chapter 5
Trapped

I couldn't stay awake anymore. Inside my room, I plonk onto my bed and fall asleep.

When I wake up, I can't remember where I am. It is bright in the room as the lights were not switched off when I slept. I'm standing on some brown boxes while on my left are rows of empty book shelves. Then I recognise the boxes are actually the television cabinet with its doors and drawers closed. The book shelves are the wardrobe I have not yet hung my clothes in. Without trying, I have deduced I am lying on my bed. I've a sudden realisation I am in America, and then the present (past and future) dawn in my mind.

I'm still in the clothes I wore to King's Junior, and above me – no longer in front – the glow in the ceiling recess throws a bright orange on my body. The digits on the face of the silent radio shows four thirty in the morning, and gaps between the double curtains show darkness still commanding the streets.

I want to do something, but I am in no mood to do anything. I wouldn't have felt so cold, if something eaten is left in my stomach. I turn off the air conditioning and drag myself into the bathroom for a hot shower. The warm water is such a relief I stay under it till my body cries to be taken out, and the steam gets too heavy on my lungs. I would like to continue hiding here, but I can't. I step over the side of the bathtub and stand in front of the rectangular mirror fitted to the wall above the basin. I towel my body, and I comb my hair.

In the large mirror, attached with two side ones, is a long body showing an insipid cage. Below the cage are a misanthropic tube and two desiccated pouches sagging from a mouldy clump. I'm surprised to recognise this inane object staring back at me with two glossy stones.

In desperation, I broaden my bloodless face with a lifeless grin. Two pale pink slabs turn instantly into an abalone body with white flakes of skin. I stifle a laugh to climb onto the basin top. Placing my knees between the china hollow, I observe one cheek, a slanted eye, and a white nose squashed against the grotesque face of a monster on the cold mirror. Mist daubs the mirror where the mouth is like a dollop of vomit. A single ridiculous thought has brought me so far.

I couldn't find what I want and lower myself carefully onto the floor. For some time, I stand there, gazing into the mirror in front again, and into the two narrow, attached ones turned slightly inwards on my left and my right. In the mirror in front, the nose curves to the right at the bridge, before turning back. Inside this mirror in front, in the reflection of the left mirror, my left profile is different from the right profile in the right mirror in the mirror in front. I prefer the latter profile.

I look askance in front of me inside the mirror, at both sides of my face: turning them slightly each side, and confirm they are different from each other. The oblique view of the right cheek is somewhat bulky, firm and fleshy. The right curve at the nose makes the nose and the side of the face look broad and gentle. The left oblique view of the left cheek exposes a longish, sunken face with a nose that is long, thin and sharp.

Am I making it up? Am I exaggerating?

An ugly person cannot dwell on himself. An underdog has to get out and keep going. I'm relieved to find myself in this state of mind. Now, it is easy to forget my body.

I walk out of the bathroom and look at the mirror, mounted against the toilet wall outside. In this dim corridor leading to the room itself, my face is flattish and brown, and the nose (just below its bridge to the tip), appears pressed to one side. I want to go to the desk by the window, and look into the mirror above it, to compare the image there with this one. But surely, I already know how I would look like in that mirror.

The more I have, the more I need. I imagine I'm dry and stringy like a dying tree with a hump poking out on one side of my hunched back. My forehead is badly dented and bald on the right side. Flat hair with streaks of white and gaps which expose pink flesh is combed straight down on the other side. Sticking out like a tongue towards the left is my swollen lower lip.

A slanted nose is common among people with high noses. But this irregularity gives my face an air of mystery and uniqueness. How could I be so stupid to believe it makes me ugly? Objects need not be regular in shape to look good. Irregular shapes have their own charm. The idea of beauty having to be regular is a false notion. There are many proofs I'm handsome, and in their heart of hearts, people know it. Those ugly feelings about me are delusions in my head. Then I find myself becoming afraid because at any time, I would begin to feel uglier and uglier.

My mind is moving beyond control. Now I want to be ugly again because of the security it brings. A man without anything loses nothing. I can't concentrate if I am handsome; I can't live freely when I know I am handsome. How could I be free if I've to protect my looks and also the evidence?

The room is bright now with the morning light breaking through the gaps. I feel hunger gnawing at the lining of my stomach. The "bag" is bloated, and I belch uncontrollably. After a few times, I feel better. I'm about to put on my undergarments when I think I should eat something to prevent gastric ulcers. I chomp some crackers, and the crumbs fall on my naked body and sting it. I sweep them away with my bare hands, and they attack me more. I pour water from a bottle down my parched throat. Relieved from thirst, I lie on the bed and pull the blanket over my cold feet. I get up, open the TV cabinet in front of the bed and take the remote lying on the side. I return to the bed, switch on the TV and press the control buttons until I see Constant News Network on the screen.

The Dow Jones has fallen seventy points! A massive drop! Immediately, my mind changes direction, and I pick up the phone. I weigh the cost of a long-distance call against the need to sell the stocks. I am in no mood to decide, though this is very urgent. I replace the handset with a click.

I need to have a warped face. The monster should be obese as well so that it's not just ugly, it would be an amorphous mess without personality. Being fat and ugly can be uglier and more attractive than being thin and ugly. I see Zhu Ba Jie in front of me, but I've to be worse than him. I become more obese than someone I often imagine in depressive moments. His waist is three times his droopy shoulders, and two lumps hang like duck eggs from his bloodless cheeks. A thick flap of flesh overlaps a huge bulgy eye on one side while a tiny, double-lid eye cannot close itself on the other.

It's hard to believe this man is uglier and fatter than Zhu Ba Jie. His facial parts just refuse to come together when I need them to. I've to believe his image is absolutely monstrous, or else I can't think how ugly I am. I must force myself hard to accept his ugliness, but the acceptance always seem to come only after confusing thoughts – as though it is only an afterthought.

I can't bear the stuffiness in the room anymore. Or is it my own mind that I cannot bear? My legs are stiff with tension, so I have to drag myself to the huge box next to the wall, on the floor. I push the red button on it, and the machine chortles violently and blows hot dry air at my startled face. I wince, as I turn the knob in one swift movement, to the other end of the blue line. The air turns swiftly cold, numbing my fingers.

Suddenly, I am filled with superiority and prestige. The cumbersome gifts try to break out of my brain like hot mustard. Acceptance is the only way I know which may tame this sweet but terrible beast. I tell myself I'm a genius. I try to remember having written a few masterpiece novels. I'm a celebrated painter. I am a world-class runner, an all-style Olympic swimmer and a karate black-belt champion. On reservist duty, I have the role of a commando general. I'm equal to Emperor Qin Shi Huang who first united China. But I am more than that. I'm the god of gods.

Nothing is greater than me. My glory stretches into the tip of the sky. I pull the curtains apart and look skywards. It is bright out there beyond the peak of the tallest building, among skyscrapers. I accept my greatness with humility. I never fight for glory. Glory is a great thing to have, but I have it from the very beginning. (I don't really want to be a god. I only want to be as great as he or she is, so that I can practise humility like a god. How can I be humble as a god if I don't believe I am a god? Alas, I have to want it!)

Then, I feel that is still not good enough. I try to be everything, and be humble. I have to accept this new greatness which has nothing greater. I try to feel as though I don't even have to accept it because I never feel it's anything great.

***

It must be lunch time. I want to get out and roam the streets for some food and fresh air, but I still can't move. The newsreader announces, with practised sadness on her face, the dead body of a young and pretty student was found at Pershing

Square after being raped. My attention was relentlessly sucked away by the TV screen.

After the carnival last night, the student stayed on in the secluded area and a group of men appeared and spoke to her. Suddenly, they covered her mouth and pulled the struggling body into a truck. The lustful objects ripped off objects covering her. Flesh wanted flesh! Flesh turned against flesh. Bodies and minds rape a body and mind.

The girl's pictures are shown in succession on the screen. It tells the story of a life before destruction ends it. She was once a normal-looking toddler. She became sexy and beautiful, and wore fashionable and revealing clothes. Then suddenly, her life was squelched out of her body like a cockroach's after being ruthlessly used. Her body and soul will disappear altogether. Beautiful or ugly, great or humble, happy or depressed; there is no difference.

Her story is revealed over millions of televisions in different places at one time. It'll be repeated again and again as the pictures flicker all over the universe like the tiny stars in the sky. More than the millions of people "watch" these screens. The girl's face will be eked into minds, and she may be a recurring feature in the consciousness of all sorts of beings.

I remember this place is crime infested as sirens reverberate in my head. I heard the wails throughout the night; but only now, I'm aware of them. If not for this accident, I wouldn't remember it at all, and those wails would have stayed out of me forever.

Every event is important and effective as it causes the next one.

I know I'm getting nowhere. I walk up and down the room. The dirty matted beards on the white carpet make my bare feet itchy. I look down at my naked chest and consciously watch my legs changing places to induce calmness. I lie on the bed and fall quickly into a dreamless sleep.

When I wake up, I try to leave the room, but my mind is too clouded. It has to be cleared first: at least, most of it. Like those out-of-body experiences during sleep when one struggles hard to get up, at some point, my body begins to move.

My eyes wander to the TV screen. An armoured tank with a soldier on top appears, and disappears. The newsreader appear from inside again.

***

I return to the bathroom to look in the mirror. Everything is where it was before. The wet cloth lies on the floor, still in front of the toilet bowl. The cubicle is a good place to think.

In the mirror on my left is my full-face reflection of the mirror in front. There is more depth – and more life – in this face than the one in front of me. The same state exists on the face in the right mirror which is another reflection of the full face in the front mirror. I feel uneasy over something I hope as usual to think away.

Both left and right faces look different from the face in front. In both the left and right mirrors, the full-face reflections of the image in the mirror in front of me (facing me) show the facial features at the same places as they appear in flesh. These positions would also be found on my faces in photographs, except the image in the mirror in front actually shows a reverse left-right reflection of my real face.

The picture in the left mirror is an improvement on the image in front, but something is ghastly wrong with the face in the right mirror.

I hurry into the room. I remove my crew pass from my jacket lying over the open bag on the floor. I rush back to the toilet, and face the photograph against the mirror in front of me.

I look into the left and right mirrors again. Inside these mirrors, the reflections of the photograph in the front mirror also show the same depth and life as my face would be in the flesh. The face of the photograph in the mirror in front of me, as well as those in the left and the right mirrors belong to one another; yet, once again, they are obviously different from one another. It is this dissimilarity which I cannot get used to while the reflection of the photograph in front of me, inside the front mirror, is normal and boring. The face in the right mirror which reflects the one in the front mirror, seems to be hopelessly warped as in the previous reflection of my face.

These distortions don't affect normal people and those with regular faces. Why am I always different! Does my abnormal face cause strange thoughts and problems – or have the strange thoughts and problems distorted my face? Both cases are possible, but which one started first?

A person has to take good care of his or her body, as well as the picture representations. He has to protect his prestige and the factors that contribute to "good" things as well. This is a heavier burden than physical wealth. I'm lucky my pass is laminated; otherwise, my photo would have been damaged through unavoidable carelessness. I would then try to find good reasons but at the end, blame myself. Of course, there is damage to the plastic cover which affects the way the picture looks. I can't deny this is irreversible. It also affects the photograph inside the protection as well.

Gathering my willpower, I smile to produce two deep dimples, one on each cheek. A smaller dimple sits above the one on the left cheek. This arrangement is natural and classic except if I do something or think of anything (including the dimples), the dimples would fade or disappear.

I should get a camera and have a picture of these looks taken. The trouble is whenever one was about to be taken, the look would seem artificial and the dimples less than ideal. Something always went wrong when the camera was about to click as related and unrelated thoughts surfaced. They caused disturbances and distorted my face even though I did my best not to allow them to happen. Once taken, I couldn't change or discard a picture because the image is mine – perhaps me.

The phone rings. I can't pick it up without interrupting my train of thoughts. I don't want my thoughts to lose momentum when I return to them. It won't be easy to find the point I left and restart from there. Most probably, I'll not even be able to remember what I was thinking. I could write it down, but what to write is a distraction, and the whole process takes lots of time. I would also forget what I mean if I write too detailed. I've the feeling a headache is developing.

The phone rings again. I should do what I want and disregard less important things, but I can't. I think I shouldn't be inconsiderate. What will people say? I can tell them I wasn't in the room when the phone rang, but who would believe that? The problem is once I pick up the phone, my pursuit of the truth would be in disarray. Events and thoughts would take me away from my intended path. No one can touch me if I make them wait, but an invisible effect on the mind directs me. I pick up the phone, my hand shaking.

The sweet, familiar voice sounds apologetic. "I have been calling. Sorry to disrupt your sleep? I ordered two portions of Thai food. One is your dinner. Please come to my room."

"I'll go over once I dress up."

I put on my clothes and pick up my key. I am happy I didn't think much over the offer, but I am also very disappointed that I didn't think more before accepting it.

***

Her room is on the same floor, on the other side of the elevator. I walk to the end of the corridor but couldn't recall the number. Quickly, I retrace the steps to the door with the "Do Not Disturb" sign, and hoping I am right, insert the key.

"Who's that?" a voice I can't recognise asks.

I apologise immediately and hurry to the door opposite the cleaning trolley. I push in my key. I only remember vaguely this is my room. To my relief, I could turn the key and push the door open. I ran to the desk, fumble with the papers and found the crew list. As I hold it against the table light, my finger moves down and locates "Sarah Tan". I mumble the number next to the name repeatedly as I trot to her room.

Panting, I knock on the door.

"Who's that?" It's her voice this time.

I stand thinking, *who am I?* I realise I can't remember my name with confidence. My name is Liu Xiang. They call me "Liu", but now those words seem so remote and uncertain. "Liu Xiang" doesn't ring. Neither does "Xiang". I repeat in my mind: *Xiang, Liu Xiang.* The more I repeat them, the more unsure I become.

"Liu," I stammer.

"Wait a minute. I'm coming." The door opens. I expect to see an unhappy face with a curl of irritation on the lips. Instead, there is a beam on her face and an anxious edge in her voice. "You take so long. They have all left."

"I'm sorry. I won't disturb you a moment longer. Once I have paid …"

"You stay here and eat. Can? What have you been doing?" Her voice is friendly and warm: just what I need!

"I'm very tired. I lost the way."

"Stay here and talk." She walks past me, and closes the door gently. There is purposefulness in her movements. "Are you sure you're okay?"

I want to talk. I need company but only for a while. I sit, disoriented, in front of the round table, while she pulls the chair behind the desk to sit opposite me.

"How much are the noodles?"

"Finish eating first, then ask me."

"But I think I should leave you alone."

"Don't you have something better to say to me? You look like you have been drinking."

I don't know what to say which would interest her. I shall tell her what is troubling my mind. It's difficult to explain, so I try something simple.

I rest my knotty hand on the table. Five long digits, all segmented, join the dorsal side of the crouching palm. Greenish veins travel on the dark surface and crawl under the blue sleeve. I turn the animal over to reveal a pink underbelly with limbs scratching the air.

"What's this?"

"Your hand."

"I can't see it's a hand. And why is it mine?"

"Of course it's a hand! And it's your hand."

I am surprised at her open mind. "How do you know?"

"Xiang!" She touches the back of my hand with delicate fingers, her sharp nails poking the sensitive surface. "See, that's your hand. You can feel it. You feel my hand. You know they're both hands." Her hand linger on top of mine, reluctant to move away, as though it's another animal.

"Why?"

"There's no why. It's a hand and nothing else."

I look at her pretty face. I couldn't understand why it's there. Why do they call it "Sarah", when they see it? Why is Sarah looking at me tenderly?

I prise the lid off the plastic box clumsily and pull apart the chopsticks attached together. She pulls open the stapled top of a tiny bag and gently shakes out pieces of green chilli onto my food.

"Here's a serviette. Hold it with your hand and use it to wipe away the crumb on your chin."

"Thanks. Something white. Why must I hold it with my hand?"

"I tell you, it is a serviette and that's your hand. Full stop!" She sounds impatient, but she is smiling, full of kindness and sympathy. "Come on, Xiang, don't worry so much. I like men like you. So sensitive."

I eat while she places her dainty hand on my thigh, the deliciousness oozing through the porous cloth.

"Come on. Don't worry about a hand."

"Hand," I whisper to myself. The word sticks there. I close my eyes and repeat the word in my mind. *Hand* remains frozen – refusing to move.

I know I can't get into a relationship with anyone. It has happened a few times. I am full of ideas on the first meetings; yet after the second ones, I would've nothing to say. I would want to be alone, keep myself company and comb through the various problems. It always seemed the problems would eventually end, but they never did.

I shan't waste her time as well as mine. My desire is pushing painfully against the fabric, but my mind cries out loud for clarity and relief at the same time. I have only finished half my noodles as I replace the lid on the box. Then I put the box and the broken chopsticks into the plastic bag.

"See you next time." I stand to leave. She stands too, smiling, hiding her disappointment. I feel sorry for her.

"Okay, then. Call me when you want to talk."

I leave the room, confused.

***

The feeling exists as heaviness in my heart while a vague form clogs my head. I tell myself I am weak – and wrong again. After all, I was aware I could be making a mistake when I told Sarah I would go to her room. Regret happens again and again, making me feel I only lose.

Once I enter my room, I close the door and turn around. I want to go straight to my desk and write – but at the entrance to the bathroom, I step over the doorsill. I stand in front of that mirror above the basin. This time, the image is covered in close-fitting jeans and a shirt from the neck down. I don't know why I am here. I ask what I've been thinking since I left my room. I can't remember the sequence, but I know what I haven't thought or done.

I look into the right mirror, at the image reflected from the front mirror. I look at my left "oblique" focusing on the shoulder and chest. It is flattish and somewhat fragile. This side is quite all right with clothes on but will look really pitiful if I remove those covers. I look at the left mirror for right "oblique". The shoulder and chest on the right side of my body are muscular – different from those of the left.

I leave the bathroom by stepping over the doorsill, and walk to that tall mirror in the dim corridor. Oblique views here don't show much without other mirrors to reflect it.

I turn my body around so that the back faces the mirror. I turn my head and strain my eyes to look at the reflection. Only the back of my waist and legs can be seen. Opening my legs apart, I bend down and look through the triangle. In the mirror, my upside-down face is flushed red, the cheeks are chubby and the flesh collects at the cheekbones. The forehead bulges with veins popping out on three sides. My hair falls sideways from the ears.

I stand up, turn around and look at my face in the mirror. I bend my waist (and face) to the right, and my face becomes a fat mango, with the right cheek drooping towards the floor. I do the same on the left. The hair on the left side of my face falls downwards this time, and the nose bends awkwardly due to the right curve at the bridge.

If I have another mirror with me, I'll place it just above my forehead but look into the mirror in front. Then, it will reveal an unbloated face even though it's upside down – unlike the one seen between my legs.

Returning to the bathroom, I kick the floor cloth away. I pull and push the door till the mirror mounted on it faces that mirror above the basin. Facing the door mirror, I look at the reflection of the mirror on the wall. I'm glad my back is smart and trim from the head to the knee.

I can't decide which the best image is and which is real, when they're all real. I want the real stuff, and I want the best. I want the best for the truth, but the best also depends on how creative one is. To be creative is to cheat. I can't prevent others from cheating, so I should join them. Does creativeness really have a hand in what is true? I can't think of anything which hasn't "cheated".

Walking and standing makes my legs strong, but they are now tired and sore. I'm about to walk out of the bathroom to think out my problems on the bed, when I hold on to the round magnifying mirror (attached to the side wall above the basin top). I twist it to face me like a monkey does. When I lower my head, my forehead enlarges, and my face becomes a standing bulb. I move back, face up slightly and there is an hourglass. My face moves back still, and it turns into a gourd.

When my face nears the magnifying mirror, the image grows more than twice. Pimple holes become black and very clear. A thumb and a forefinger unite, and the natural tweezers squeeze the sides of a hole. Near the nose tip, a long-looking white substance protrudes horizontally, drooping a little.

Reluctantly, I rub the cheesy excrescence out of existence and move my fingers to make another. A hump bursts at times and fire jets of viscous liquid at the mirror. Soon, red patches cover my nose, making it look like an onion bulb. I tell myself any damage is temporary, and that the skin is really being cleansed, yet I find myself already loving it.

My heavy hands take a face towel and wet it after turning on the tap. They are forced to the oily mirror and wipe off the yellowish spots.

I step over the doorsill and drag myself into the shrinking room. It compresses me, and I feel I'm going to explode. The TV produces giddy images and jarring noises. I snatch the remote on the mattress and press the red button many times. As the screen flashes, the bright light explodes and reverses into a dot. I feel better when the TV becomes a dead box.

In this state of mind, a yawn leaks as I carry my attaché case to the mattress. I pull the chair and the rubbish bin from the desk to the side of the bed. I sit on the chair and unfold the bag into two sides, one side standing at right angle to the horizontal side.

The bag is full of stuff jumbled together and jutting out of the pockets on the vertical side. Bits of paper and tiny balls of dust hide at the base. Most of the circulars, old and frayed at the edges, shouldn't be here anymore. I hold a stack of circulars to look for something to throw away.

Some circulars are still relevant while a few have not even been read. They are issued regularly, and there is one which holds my attention. Circular dated March 15, 1979: passengers would no longer be given free cigarettes. So that's why we have not been distributing cigarettes for some time, but it wouldn't have made any difference to me if I knew. (I force myself to accept this.) The rest are even more uninteresting, As I don't need these circulars, I slide the stapled stacks into the waiting bin.

I feel lighter throwing all that away. Eventually the housekeeper will take the bin and throw its contents into the bag hanging on one side of her trolley. The rubbish would be sent somewhere and put out of existence (or recycled).

I rest my head on two pillows. I recall the sliding sounds made by the paper on the bin.

I wake up a short while later. It's dark outside. Sarah didn't even call me. I've wasted an opportunity to have a beautiful experience with her and maybe, there was a hidden lesson in it as well. You can't have the apple and eat it, but I seem to have ended with nothing again. I hope she will call. My hand moves to the telephone on the side table and picks up the handset. Then I replace it on the cradle.

I put on my blazer. I wear my shoes. I'm determined to go for a walk: for fresh air and dinner. The air conditioning has made the room very dry and very soon, the restaurants would close.

I walk to the toilet and face the mirror to comb my hair. I scrape my scalp, and an avalanche of white glitter falls onto the dark jacket. I look at the white existents in awe as though snow has fallen suddenly onto the ground. I comb my hair across the scalp again, this time noticing the sharp and painful sensation. More blessed white flakes! Soon, the fall dwindles to mere droplets floating down casually each time I comb. I look at my shoulder on the right where the white is most striking. I look in the mirror. I want to clear the snow or flip my jacket in the air, but how can I wipe existence away!

Carefully, I remove the jacket and hang it in the cabinet.

***

I remember I still have half an uneaten lunch. In silence, I pick the soggy strands of noodles with broken chopsticks and deliver them to my dry mouth. My hands shake as I gulp down water and carry the chair back to the desk. I sit, bend over the desk.

I wonder if I should write. I have written so much I've forgotten where they are. I wouldn't be able to find most of the stuff when I eventually look for them, though I cling to the belief they're safe somewhere. Some stuff began in notebooks but ended up on scraps or pieces of paper. These were left wherever I felt was convenient and recoverable. Sometimes, I wrote letters with carbon papers and kept the copies when I sent the originals. Recently, I wrote mostly on foolscap. The feeling is much of what I wrote has been lost or thrown away by people. Bits and pieces often appeared out of nowhere.

I think I am wasting precious time worrying since everything is naturally looked after. I'm not fickle-minded when I say this, but I'm truthful. Obviously, my mind has shifted again, and wavering concentration causes bad understanding. I have to accept this usually happened.

Yet I've always continued writing. It's evidence that, at least once, I walk on this earth. Writing records the way I exist, is my proxy and actually preserves the self. The rich used to store their well-preserved remains in opulent mausoleums, while capable souls fought or provided service to make names for themselves for posterity.

I first started writing to have a record to compare the present with the past – and plan for the future. I used it to track changes in me and took note when I stayed the same. I hoped to distil vital truths from my history in the notes. Then, I could find what I might or might not wish to change.

When I wanted to postpone thoughts, I also wrote. Small notes left on the table or pinned to the board ended up between the pages of school books. Unfortunately, some were even pushed between objects or under them. The practice was itself "hung up" for another time, when I felt I hadn't pursued postponed matters with determination.

I write so I won't forget feelings and thoughts which sneaks by, observations I made on the go and conclusions formed intuitively. I write because impressions made under unique circumstances are difficult to come by again and very likely to be forgotten.

I write quickly so as not to disrupt my thought process. I think and write – and think again. I don't want to do that too often. I don't want what is written to be different from what it should be, and it then affects my life and thinking. I don't like to think and write, or to live and write, at the same time. Like the practice of awareness, they would alter the natural process of living.

I wrote many things so quickly my writing soon became illegible. I then took steps to write legibly, but when my writings were legible, I still couldn't understand most of what I wrote since I had forgotten what they actually meant. Legibility, clarity and substantiation are difficult issues to handle in a hurry.

I wrote immediately after, I wrote soon after, and I wrote long after something happened. When I am happy, it's difficult to find the wish to write, but when I am sad or depressed, I can't write either. This excessive reliance of moderate moments to write and think, I fear, may not treat the truth fairly.

I can't write about what I have just been through. Those very thoughts make me sick. I'm worried once I write, I will get the same thoughts again. Of course, they're going to show up all over again, but it'll be another time during which I hope I will be able to deal with them in the right frame of mind.

My memory is slowly but surely losing clarity through the years. I have to write thoughts down before they become disconnected, or I lose them completely.

Chapter 6
1955: Frustrations

My family shared the dark kitchen with the landlord and other tenants. The walls were sooty and the floor was wet, but the blackened pots and pans sat neatly on a dry cement top. On the other side of the kitchen, sitting on another top were portable clay stoves we took turns to use. In the background, I would hear the shushing sounds of clothes being scrubbed by hand against a corrugated washing board. Grown-ups thrust firewood through an opening in front of the stoves to feed hungry flames swallowing the pots from below. A woman scooped water from a big ceramic pot patterned with dragons into a zinc tub for me to bath in. On cold days, she poured steaming water from a sooty kettle and mixed it with chilly water. This woman who washed my naked body and caused the shushing sounds was definitely my mother.

All this was real except that one day an old grandmother figure I never saw before, appeared in the same dark kitchen. She appeared to be in her seventies which was very old age at the time. Swiftly she came down the spiral staircase, in a pair of grey, wide traditional trousers and a blouse. Her hair streaked almost entirely with white, was combed neatly to the back. She appeared to be my grandmother, yet I know none of my grandparents ever left China, and I only saw those on my mother's side in a yellowed photograph. She dashed across the kitchen in front of me and disappeared. This was the earliest period in my life I remember, beyond which was emptiness. I was then probably less than two years old, though the feeling was no different from that during adulthood. I couldn't remember being inside a womb or something similar. And I've never been sure whether the old woman was a real person, a ghost or a dream.

There was one incident around that time which appears more realistic. After dinner when darkness fell, I often sat with both my tiny legs tucked through the gaps of the wooden railing below the casement window of our single room. On the dark street, one floor below, bicycles and cars rang and honked as they weaved their way through the chatty crowds. Hawkers howled their wares, the smell of food wafted through the gaps, and a man in white came dragging a long sack which trailed him over his shoulder. He was crying out something I didn't understand even as objects inside the sack wailed loudly into the vibrant, humid night. My sisters were standing around me, I think, as someone explained the man bought kids from parents who sold them because they were naughty. But the bag of children remains an illogical feature in my mind.

These two lucid events hover between the unreal and the real within my memory. After this, events were more realistic but not necessarily clearer. Hot, prickly pain seared my mind whenever I remembered the heat rash practically covering my entire body. There were attacks of disgust followed with nausea whenever I was conscious of the appearance, taste and smell of food as it made its way into my mouth and alimentary canal. I was gripped by crippling insecurity whenever I saw the rice stock dwindle to the base of the aluminium tub and could only hope my father would be able to replenish it. I can't forget stalls down the road at night where cat and mouse games were played by unlicensed street vendors and customs officers. Cries of panic and shouts of triumph arose out of the market cacophony when men and women took down their stalls and fled. The fragrance of chicken soup and the obnoxious smell of carbide waltzed around orange and blue flames flickering on tall thin stems.

My favourite haunt was the spartan toilet at home where I squatted astride the oval receptacle. Theories were found in the solitude, as many others were eliminated. I met hardworking and stoic ants who ran nonstop on the floor and climbed the walls. I saw their commitment and contribution when they stacked cargoes of food with skill and professionalism in return for benefits.

A spotted beige marble rolled on the uneven mat in my room and made a crackling noise whenever it hit another hard ball. Both marbles wobbled away from each other, after that. A small hole on the surface – which had lost its lustre as days went by – grew into a deep irregular crater with the same cragginess all the time. There were feelings of solidity and cold when I held the sphere in my hand and examined the mysterious hole. Something beyond function, about the form and other qualities, defied my conceptualising mind – suggesting a personality which followed the object everywhere.

There was strange familiarity in myself. My legs and the muscles changed shapes when they moved, but I could recognise them. My hands stayed with me day and night, everywhere I went, followed by their shadows. My hands and feet felt strange, and felt strange things. Different objects had similar as well as different features and a way of establishing their presence. They didn't push their way in, and they weren't sneaky. Everything was suspicious as though I should throw them all away, yet those hands and legs were mine, and real.

I found myself thinking of accumulation, but it didn't begin outside me. I saw how food enter and become part of my body which, I felt was me. But my bodily mass couldn't be only increasing, as I would've become very large. Adults would be giants with very different heights and sizes. I was losing myself when I saw sweat, tears and blood, hair and skin, and urine and faeces fall away and never return. I was throwing away parts of myself when I visited barbers, and I cut my nails.

I saw something called balance. That was why as I gained mass, I was losing it too. My body needs balanced food and exercise to be strong and healthy. Bones and muscles have to be burdened, while reflexes and the mind need constant challenges. Emotions have to be tempered. Nothing should be overdone or there is destruction. I never acquired the joy of accumulating wealth since I knew I would lose it all – like my mass. But *success, fame and greatness* were stirring as they could protect and promote that familiar mass.

Since I couldn't protect my body from gradual loss, I looked for something that stays. My attention turned to the hardy parts of my body, but one after another, I gave up any hope of their permanence. My bones, teeth, nails and hair – I finally admitted – were all temporary.

Before I began school, I would imagine wearing thick, ironclad armour as though I were General Guan Yu. His picture card was normally the one inside little boxes popular with children who bought the dried fruit pieces. Swinging a halberd, I found myself knocking away arrows flying all around at Liu Bei and me. I carried swords and axes, fought with the valiant Zhang Fei by my side, and won fights and battles. When we moved to a fifth-storey flat in the suburbs, I imagined myself in a massive tank, the size of our seven storey block, rumbling down the tarmac road. I was often on rescue missions and made enemies. They came for my life now and then, but were never a match for my men and me in the impenetrable tank. I stood on the balcony to direct battles, survey enemies or negotiate. I became concerned one day I might be shot at, so I put on more armour though I was always inside the "fortress".

In fact, I began school at seven. A flattish piece of rubber was given out, along with a long ruler and two pencils, to all the children on the first day. From that moment, the new arrival was a presence every day – with the softness whenever I squeezed it. Sometimes the bluish eraser lay on the grey table, sometimes on top of my exercise book, but it always caused anxiety and excitement. I was drawn to it despite feeling it was somehow faking its presence and up to something. Once it was shut inside the pencil case a few times daily, it seemed to return to nonexistence, and I would be rueful but at ease.

There was a short aggressive boy in my class during Primary One. He claimed to be protected by a supernatural power and often threatened others with his professed power. To get even, I imagined training till my body was like iron, then soaking it in a powerful fluid for more strength and empowerment. When I was living in the house where I saw the man with the long sack, there was a kindly old medium living a few doors from ours. He would cut his tongue on festive occasions and used the blood to write paper talismans. Sometimes, I carried a paper talisman in my purse and felt that no gun or knife could penetrate my body. I also felt no accidents could harm me, and I was protected from invisible forces.

We played police and thief in school and hurled rubber balls at each other. Since every hit by a solid ball was excruciating, I wore two T-shirts beneath my starched and ironed uniform. I added another layer to feel more invincible, but it was so hot one afternoon in the July equatorial sun, I gave up the idea forever. So I became Robin Hood in light clothing, roving in the forest. I leaped and twisted like the kung fu heroes in comics, to avoid rocketing balls in school. There were successes, as well as accidents which caused nausea and my head spun at fantastic speed when I lay flat. I thought I might have brain damage which compromised my perception.

My mind often wandered away in class to think about vague matters, though I didn't try to find out what they were. I would be singled out for inattention and poor progress so that for a few days before an examination, I had to mug up late into the night.

I was in Primary Three, when I was reading a book. Towards the end of it, one of the two birds died. I became aware time is always on the move and is unstoppable. Each moment, I was closer to the moment when I would leave this world. I couldn't take life as it was anymore. Every second, I was aware of death closing tighter on me, though I could do something limited to prolong my life without certainty. It seemed to me and I knew I was right, life was moving inexorably towards death and the realisation of this continuous movement immobilised me. It was futile to do anything for myself anymore. I might as well end it right away, or enjoy life to the full and wait for the moment of death. I began my search for immortality. Then I realised I didn't even know who I was.

I first thought of myself as a body. Straightaway, I had trouble, since every moment I'm losing parts of my body. I identified myself with my blood, but there was no difference. Then I thought I was a ghost, then a soul. But nothing could be held on to. They all slipped away upon scrutiny.

I consoled myself with the idea of essence. Whatever happened to my body, something which doesn't have to be physical, would be unaffected. Essence, in fact, is a better type of permanence. Blood or the brain failed the grade because they were constantly changing, while the mind was even more fleeting. Blood, and plausibly the brain could also be transferred to another person. I tried ideas of soul and spirit and ghost, and thought of being only a point or an existent. But none of these concepts qualify as essence, as they were endlessly reducible and not at all permanent. A point could always be reduced to a smaller point.

I tried to encounter ghosts and experience the paranormal. This would go in some way to prove the presence of the essence. But I took ghost stories apart to see if they were genuine. Miracles and supernatural events were dissected and scrutinised. To my dismay, I was always able to show that those fantastic claims were not infallible.

At the end, the realisation dawned on me that even the existence of the supernatural doesn't negate the problems of personal existence. There is no difference between the material and the spiritual worlds. Form is emptiness, emptiness is form. No single state is better than the other. To accumulate spiritual merits is like material greed. I didn't know whether to be happy or sad about it.

I told myself, perhaps, I should transfer my vague longing to lineage, humanity or the world – something else I was related to and could identify with. I could even try God or Gods, existence or isness. I should identify with something outside myself and work for it. Then I thought it didn't matter whether I was part of anything. Maybe, I could be disinterested in identity. I found that isness has nothing to do with longing. It was meaningless clinging to identity.

So I'm merely a composite. I don't really exist. "I" exists only because conditions exist. Yet do conditions exist by themselves? At the end, the all-important questions: Is there existence and inexistence? Is existence something and inexistence nothing? Is there nothing? Is there something? Can I exist when it is nothing? The fundamental question: what is existence? Yet it does not matter! Nothing matters!

One day, I was engrossed in some matters when suddenly, I realised I still didn't have the answers to basic questions like who I was. I couldn't focus on unrelated matters anymore. Without absolute certainty nothing was wrong with life, I couldn't allow myself to live freely. I searched for answers inside and outside myself until I felt I found them, or I was too tired. I checked conclusions from every angle. I stopped whatever I was thinking or doing, to check them against every situation. When an answer was found wanting, it was reexamined. If I couldn't remember the answers clearly, the process had to be repeated. I would've a respite if I got caught up with what was happening around me.

At first, I could postpone thoughts to attend to urgent matters without providing reasons. Then, I had to give reasons. Finally, those had to be good reasons. Sometimes, on continuing what I was thinking previously, I couldn't remember where I stopped, or what the answers I thought I found were. I wrote what I needed to remember on paper, but there were new problems.

The golden liquid from that brittle bottle on the dining table filled up the glass with a layer of undulating white froth on top. The beer entered one of the two dreamlike bodies conversing in Fuqing, seated on the chairs and contributed to its glory. I was allowed only one sip because I was still young. The positive liquid thrilled me as it coursed down inside my absorbent body, and I thought of the value added.

That fountain pen sucked blue ink from a mottled bottle on the desk. The colour and smell of the translucent liquid evoked fascination. As the nib was pushed on the white paper, the ink leaked out and formed blue shapes of different sizes. It was somewhat scary this was possible. Once the liquid dried up, and its presence in another form on paper was permanent, it was magic. Yet nothing is magic or a miracle. There could only be science, most of which we didn't understand.

I fashioned pieces of used wood into two crude bookstands and arranged books between them. I borrowed books from the library and stood them next to mine. I skimmed through a few passages of the borrowed books quickly, but engrossed myself most of the time with their physicality. The printed words and the feel of paper lived in my confused and elated mind. My hands shifted the bookstands constantly to touch the objects I brought into existence. It was a relationship between objects and their creator.

I never had true happiness. The island was transformed into a prosperous and modern city with tall buildings very quickly. I hadn't been mistreated during childhood, and there was no lack of love; yet whenever there was happiness, it was always spoilt by a nagging worry it was a facade which would slip away. I was constantly aware there could be mistakes and problems regarding existence – including mine – which I couldn't point out to others without making myself appear crazy.

In desperation, I seized pleasurable moments to believe they were true happiness, and that all the vexing questions would never return. Yet, I always knew the paradise I made out of festive celebrations like Lunar New Year and the Lantern Festival, and eating delicious foods like crabs would somehow slip away. I found paradise and hell, happiness and sadness were relative states of mind which don't exist. Alas, I was right that though emotional and physical pains could be defined and managed to some extent, abstract mental pains about existence were unsolvable and would haunt me like sinister shadows forever.

One day, I looked into the mirror. I wasn't sure I was handsome or ugly, but I was fascinated. Was this another representation of me? Was this another form of existence or the same existence? I became obsessed with photographs. I took to care for them in the best possible way, and I made sure nothing positive about my body would be missed out in a photograph. Yet, I found it difficult to leave out whatever was negative. I took care not to damage each and every photograph as if it was a representation of me that would last longer than my body, and which had captured at least a moment of my being and might preserve it into eternity, if I assiduously looked after it well.

I became worried about everything that happened to my body or anything that might affect it. One reason was that any part of my body could become the subject of some photographs or drawings. I became worried about my prestige, image, health, mental state – everything about me. How interconnected everything is! …

***

I put down my pen to have a rest when there are hesitant knocks on the door. Two more soft knocks later, I hear footsteps moving away. It's almost midnight, and someone outside didn't want to disturb me if I'm asleep – although my room lights are still on. I look through the peephole and don't see anyone. As the door is chained, it's safe to open it. It is stopped abruptly by the chain.

"Liu, were you sleeping?" It is Feng's kindly, strong voice.

"No."

"What are you doing at this hour? Where did you go to, today?"

"I was in my room."

I unchain the door and open it. Feng appears, looking tired with a twinkle in his eyes. He wears a sweater over his shirt and his oiled hair is dull and frayed. Fattened plastic bags hang heavily from one hand. His other hand holds out the handle of a smaller bag for me to take.

"I was out the whole day. Did a lot. I bought a foot-long chicken sandwich as I thought you would be awake. A little extra in case you need it. I didn't buy much since we're checking out around noon."

"You're sure you've enough for yourself?"

"Of course. Tomorrow, I'll have an apple. This apple is for you."

It is a relief as I'm hungry. I ask how much the food cost, but he refuses to say and suggests I return him with a treat another time. I push two green notes from my wallet into his hand. He takes them reluctantly. I break the sandwich and return him the other half. I gobble it as I stand there.

Feng's life is well-organised, but he doesn't even plan it. He lives by his principles and responds to situations admirably. He is a thinker like me except, he is able to let thoughts go when he has to. After doing what he has to, he'd be able to return to think. He's never flustered. He goes through all sorts of situations without fear. He could do all this because he doesn't care for the absolute Truth.

There are many things I want to do and think about, but never get to do them. The opportunities are always there even when earlier ones were lost, but I could never bring myself to work on them. I kept going about life the same way, and couldn't plan for my needs. Even when something was part of my plan, I couldn't carry it out. I can't really blame myself. There are too many basic issues not resolved, and it's hard to tackle an issue before a more fundamental one has been solved. Each issue takes too long to be resolved and never seems to get solved, anyway.

To disrupt my train of thoughts or not, so that I could entertain an intrusive idea (even one which belongs to a different issue) is one of the most difficult dilemmas. No single issue is isolated, and the discovery or loss of anything would affect whatever truth I am looking for. Two or more paths: each with its own advantages and disadvantages, but there is only one to take.

I'm not sure whether to be ashamed to have depended on people like Feng. Without them, I could be roaming the streets like a mad man rummaging garbage for food. I feel useless, yet some say it's fate which decides who is privileged to be looked after. They should call it a talent.

Feng opens the bulgy bag for me. I look at the books inside with no interest but notice the author's name on a spine.

"I can't believe it. He says when one is taken out of the body, one will see it from above. One then know, he or she is not a body but a point; or a soul if you will."

"Yes, it's true. Only his trained deputies have the power to order you out of your body."

"Have you ever been taken out of your body?"

"No."

"Then you can't believe what he says. And what happens if the deputy doesn't bring you back into your body?"

"But people have left their body. People who astral travel for example," he says firmly.

"Maybe they imagine it after all the suggestions."

"He says once you experience it, you will know you're not your body. I like him. He's very scientific and exact."

"I can't say what others say is untrue because I've not experienced it. But by the same token, I can't say it is true. Even if I experienced something,

I might not agree with someone else's intellectual interpretation. They said the out-of-body experience is the same as you struggle to wake up and see your body lying there. I experienced that a few times but after finally waking up, I wasn't sure what it was. Then I thought of what people said, and realised they've only believed a theory. I've mediated in a group when members saw glitter of light fall all over the body. It gave them great joy, but I had never experienced it other than a sense of wonderful peace. Why does everybody say the same about an experience if they're from a same group? It seems they should interpret it according to their own intellect, but a member is obliged to think a certain way."

He says, "All religions are the same. They teach you to be good and to believe in God."

"People go through the same path, but every religion says it has the only Truth. Actually, those claims are based on speculation and cause serious problems. There is plenty of dishonesty in their arguments. For example, they use the logic the world has to come from something to prove God exists, but if you use the same argument to show they've created a new problem, they say He can't be understood or proved with logic. I'm not saying there is no God or He has to be created, but the premise used to prove His existence is desperate and unnecessary. A greater lie is to claim that since they have proved God's existence, their religion and all it says can only be true. Most religionists don't even know they are lying; or if they do, they are very afraid to admit it. They themselves are victims of lies which are largely beneficial in the normal sense. We've to be mindful that what is beneficial is not necessarily the ultimate Truth."

He looks at me confidently. "Scientific thinking can't go wrong."

"Science is empirical but like history, it is based on a massive collection of facts by different individuals and interests. You never know it when the so-called facts or premises are wrong especially when you're a lay person."

"You are too pessimistic? You have to be positive."

"When I was young, I used to go out with my mother after dinner to collect clothes for her to wash. It was a thirty-minute walk to the destination. Halfway, we would cross a lonely bridge with no houses nearby. I had seen a crocodile there once. In the dark I would be afraid.

"One night I thought to myself, 'Is the person walking with me for so long still my mother?' I held her hand tight and looked at her, and wasn't sure. Once, I had an idea. My mother had a mole on the right side of her nose bridge. When some light fell on it that night and I saw it, I was happy and assured; but that feeling didn't last long. On another trip, I looked for that mole again, but when I saw it, I remained in doubt.

"Then I started to have constant doubts: though I think, my doubts started even before that."

People like Feng have good control of themselves and manage the world according to their needs. They exude outward confidence and are concerned only with what is tangible. They either believe in something or they don't. Once they have chosen a path, they're likely to stay with it. Their unwavering nature comes from an inclination and a determination to stay on course. They dislike the discomfort and embarrassment of changing direction, and they don't feel guilty when they pander to this inclination. In fact, they have learnt to be proud of all that.

If someone pushes an abstract issue too deeply for their comfort, they beat around the bush. There are other openings if they didn't seize one to talk about something else. They could say something about the surroundings, ramble on the same subject or move on to discuss yet another issue. Or, a crew member may gossip: *which hostess is the latest slut?* To show they are intellectual, someone may ask if the deadly cycles in the Middle East will ever end. These people may even touch on the question you are burning to discuss deeply, yet they'll never delve into it. They play with words. *Believers become very successful. The person was previously suicidal.*

Afraid of dire consequences, they won't risk the wrath of the unknown. Frightened the truth would hurt, they would've nothing to do with it. They play safe with truth as they always play safe in life. They make the supreme mistake of thinking material life and absolute Truth are different and should be treated the same way. They resort excessively to belief and faith even when a case is obviously groundless. They hide themselves behind faith like wimpy men behind their mothers' skirts. Only if they are made to fear the consequences of what they do, will they be freed to look for the truth. Sad, but true!

They look for meaning in a meaningless world. When they couldn't find it, they cover up that meaninglessness with pretences. They apply layers upon layers of meaningless illusions upon existence, which is the simple truth. They tell themselves they are special enough to be given important roles.

They're not content to satisfy natural needs. They perform elaborate rituals over the plain and straightforward purpose of sex. They enhance and embellish their food and drink, their dwelling, clothing, and other things. They fill their lives with what they think others envy, or what the world tells them to have. They follow advertisements and campaigns, unconsciously and conscientiously. I see no need to lie or pretend, or do what the world wants. Why should there be meaning in life, or a reason for it: life which is simply life? What difference does it make whether it has meaning or not?

They don't really know what they so proudly expound, and are content to cover their inadequacy with excitement or smugness. These people gamble and shop for distraction. Work and charity provide temporary satisfaction. They win hearts, make money or get promoted, when they embark on conquests, to get relief from their confusing existence. At the wheel of an expensive car, they call you loudly. After travelling abroad, they talk about their experiences and insights amongst themselves, louder than usual. As they imagine being transformed into special devices which draw joy and meaning from empty space, they listen to good music and clever speeches. Having learnt to appreciate art, they claim there are esoteric and absolute meanings hidden in it. They face a masterpiece painting meekly, thinking the "all-knowing" artist will repay their humility with his or her insights. Their minds are used to push what they learnt deep into their being. After helping the living, they tell you to keep it secret, but whisper about their "kind" deeds to others. They go to temples and churches to feel safe. They store treasures in a future world, so they can use them to bargain for forgiveness or benefits. Or else, they indulge in simple physical distractions like drinking and sex.

***

"Harold spoke about his problems on board. He wanted me to help him solve them."

Feng's eyes focus on mine as if he is peering into my mind. I guess he sees something shifting inside. His arms rest on the sides of the armchair he is sitting on opposite, across the low table.

"He wanted my advice. If you like, we can help him sort it out together. I think you are a sincere type of person: that's why I am asking for your opinion. If you don't want to join me, it's okay. Just give your opinion but keep whatever I'm telling you to yourself."

The thought flits through my mind there would be an unnecessary disruption to my burning thoughts (a pilgrimage with pain and jubilation). Should I entertain an unrelated, worldly intrusion?

Gradually, I recover enough to say: "Tell me the problem. I'll give my opinion. After that, I'll let you know whether I can help. I'm really very busy."

"He came to my zone on the last flight and asked for me. We sat on the crew seats outside the galley. He pulled the curtain across it and when there wasn't any crew member around, he whispered."

I haven't been wrong about Feng. The fact is that he doesn't take liberty with a person. It's in him; he doesn't have to try to make it happen. He didn't make the assumption about me others often make to my indignation. They would say: "But you are so free, you look like you've nothing to do." They couldn't understand I am actually busier than others, though I seem to be doing nothing.

"You've a good reputation. A purser asking for advice from his junior is unheard of in this airline."

"He said he needs lots of money to pay friends and family members. Yet people owe him money. Debtors pretend they've no money. He has no proof against them since he trusted them when he lent the money. As for his creditors, they had made him sign on paper. Connie wants to give him the money. She's from a rich family. He refused to tell me why he owes the money. Maybe, he borrowed from loan sharks to help others.

"At the same time, he didn't want to lie and take advantage of Connie's feelings. She is merely a friend to him. And there is the other JP complicating things. Connie doesn't know he spoke to me about this, so please keep it a secret."

I ask, "Is he a bachelor?"

"He's not married. He has too many girlfriends, and he is a playboy. But he is not a bad person."

I search my mind thoroughly, for a good piece of advice.

"We can help him, but not with money. He has to say why he needs the money."

"I won't lend him any money. He didn't want my money, anyway. I think it has to do with the girl you saw in Tokyo."

I've been much focused. I like the way I switched to different topics and still concentrated. I want to help, as I want to be useful; yet, if I am writing, I would've written a lot when my mind is still undisturbed. It's rare these days for me to be in this state of mind.

I've been taken away again from my mission, and it is not as though I didn't know the tricks played on me. My mind begins to drift in despair. I doubt I should continue what I am doing. Feng's voice is a blur as I try hard to concentrate. I realise I don't know what he has just said.

"Can you repeat?"

"I said I will try to find out what's his problem and solve it. I shall stop him from borrowing money. That will only get him into deeper trouble."

"I think that's good, but I can't join you. I hope you trust me. I am very tired. I've to sleep now. You better sleep too as we are checking out later."

Feng smiles before leaving.

***

I pull the chair back to the desk. My rump fumble onto the cushioned seat. I wonder whether the momentary distraction is good for me, especially what I write. It would relieve my tired mind, and provide a window for a new perspective. Still I must avoid the trap of being mentally entangled beyond what I actually want to concentrate on. I look at where I'd stopped writing on the piece of paper and scribble a new paragraph: *My life was upside down. Every moment, I probe my mind for the answer. When I was listening to a story, I stopped. When ... eating, I stopped ... .*

I can't go on, but I try. Then I feel the pen caught within the sides of my thumb, forefinger and middle finger. I can't resist the compulsion to look at what is happening. I can't allow myself to miss it. My eyes focus for a moment on the point of contact between the tips of my thumb and my forefinger. My awareness continues to focus on this contact. It's strenuous since this awareness of contact, and the focus of writing are pulling in different directions. I am aware of the contact of the pen and two of my fingers and my thumb, between the tips of my thumb and forefinger, and between my palm and my last finger – all at the same time. It flits so fast between four poles of focus that it appears as one blob of giddy awareness. The little ache within my head sharpens.

I write: *When I went to secondary school, catching up with what I missed was difficult, but I could ...*

My rump weighs like an elephant on the chair. I feel the flattened flesh squashed painfully between the stumps at the back of my thighbone and the thinly cushioned seat. Then the lamp cable gets caught between the first and second toes of my foot, and I try to extricate my mind of it. I worry when I move my foot, I would pull the wire and maybe injure my toes.

I continue writing: ... *catch up for the examinations ...*

When I close my eyes, the contact between the upper and lower eyelids feels gummy and traps my attention. I remove my foot from the cable carefully, and pulling my sticky attention away from the distractions, I write:

I became a Christian, I realised, not because I believed ... hoped all the existential questions ... solved by the belief in God. ...

I continue to write.

***

The people who introduced me to their version of God insisted they had the only true teachings. But new problems surfaced as I grappled with the slippery concepts of His infinity. Their belief system hinged on a book I couldn't accept as what they claimed. They were unwittingly worshipping a book written about God, rather than God Himself. I didn't think I should spend my limited time on earth arguing over books, which are continuously churned out by unscrupulous men.

When I learnt to swim with the help of a book, I was struck by the fact I could only be about as good as an amphibian in water. Even if I could fly, I wouldn't be able to do it like birds or the bacteria that lived in the air as well as water. I feel I should be an all-rounder if I existed. I would be a true one if I could live on land like I was doing, swim in water like a fish and roam the sky like an eagle. Humans had longer life spans than most animals; yet if I wanted to, I wouldn't be able to live on other planets. I felt inadequate and crippled. I had no quarrels being attracted to the female sex, but I couldn't understand why I was compartmentalised into one of the sexes. Why should my body be structured to fulfil only one of the two roles for the lowly purpose of procreation? Why should I be limited to think and act according to the sex of my body? How is one's sex defined?

I found the most disruptive type of problem in my life one afternoon when I attended a meeting in a master's inner room and left my slippers temporarily outside his flat. I knew once I got involved in the discussion, I would be unaware of the slippers if I was to focus and perform. I reminded myself the footwear wasn't lining the soles of my feet anymore, and to remember to wear it on my departure. I knew of course, I wouldn't forget to wear the slippers when I was about to step out of the flat, since my bare feet needed protection outside. But something still troubled me.

Looking at it now, I could only explain I found circumstances like this deeply contradictory. I thought it was wrong for my slippers to be left outside my awareness when they were the very objects I needed to have with me, later. The slippers should be in my consciousness all the time even when they weren't with me, because I had to remember not to leave them behind. If that was not possible, at least they should be in my consciousness frequently. But what right did I have to decide the number of times those thoughts were allowed in? And what was I to do if those thoughts "forgot" to come in?

I realised the act of remembering doesn't see, (think, hear, or smell) the slippers lying outside the flat, although people would claim they knew all the time those objects are there. There is no awareness in the conscious mind of the slippers if they are not ideated, and the ideation process occurs only during moments of need. I told myself to take the risk: focus on what I could, on what I needed. Leave the slippers and other things the way they were, in the situation they were in. Allow them to exist in the state of mind I was in. Come what may!

After ejaculation, a man's body replenishes what it loses and rebuilds itself. He develops appetite and he sleeps, so that material would be made available while the body works on restoration. The body knows what to do, and it does whatever it can with what is available. If there isn't enough food or if its quality is not balanced, the body wouldn't be able to restore itself to the optimum condition. Lack of sleep and the presence of negative thoughts also result in less than optimal restoration. A similar process happens after exercise.

Moreover, if exercise is carried out before the body's full recovery from ejaculation, the body wouldn't get the full benefit from the exercise. It would be best for both the body and the mind, if none of the necessary conditions for their recovery from both the emission and exercise is lacking. If the recovery of either the body or the mind is incomplete, it would affect a person's well-being and efficiency, and even his appearance.

Ironically, it's also necessary not to worry about the recovery. One has to let go and trust nature would do whatever is necessary, if one wishes nature to perform at its best. The same rule applies if he or she wants to do anything to the best of his ability. Even if the person expects the result to be bad (or if it is, in fact, already bad), he or she has to accept it and not worry.

But the situation is never so simple. When it comes to letting go or to exercising the volition of acceptance, all sorts of permutations especially negative ones, have the tendency to present themselves.

I tried to think the right thoughts not only to induce rest, but also to help the body and the mind perform or recover, at their best. It was normal for one to try to think positive. I worried that there were too few positive thoughts, but not when there were too many of them. The more I thought positive, the stronger negative thoughts became, the more they were stirred up and they appeared in unlikely and complex ways.

Removing the source of the problem isn't a solution either. After all, ejaculation has been proved to be a source of youth and longevity.

Positive thoughts conjured to enhance other types of activities face problems too. A neutral state of mind is an important condition during a thought process. A positive or a negative mind causes skewed thinking. Yet it was impossible to clean myself of preconceptions and prejudices, even for the few moments when it was so important to do so.

It is impossible to know whether the mind was really clear of prejudice. The fact is there are always residues of prejudice. The mind never stays in a genuine state of neutrality for more than a few seconds.

I had yearned to see my name in print. When it was below a poem one day for the first time, I felt I had a spiritual experience. It was as though I was immortalised, and my existence was extended in space and time. The published poem itself gave me the same feeling of glory.

Then I wanted pictures of myself published too. Perhaps I had discovered the motivation of fame. I began to love writing, but was disheartened to find that the art was relative to different people and times. To my utter disappointment and confusion, I soon saw imperfection and much waste in the English language. I learnt that the only constant about language is change.

I canvassed for advertisements for my school's annual magazine. It revived the glorious feeling and helped me forget my troubled thoughts and the guilt of dreaming during class lessons. At the end, of course, I had felt worse. I managed to collect lots of advertisements and hoped my efforts and achievement would be duly recognised. At the end, however, it made no difference whether I collected one advertisement or most of them.

No one likes their credit given to someone else, though they wouldn't object to be given others'. I began to wish truth could never be falsified. I saw it was a real possibility, though I worried the wish compromised my integrity in the particular thought process. I thought once something happens, it is etched forever into reality. It will evolve into something else, but the original reality and what happened between then and now will never be lost. The past can always be discovered if only someone makes the right effort. This implies reality is infinite. The trouble is that too many forgeries and lies have been successfully carried out. How could I improve my looks? In other words, cheat! Not necessary! Truth is what matters. Truth is unalterable; if I cheat, it will be found out. I love to live by truth, and I love to cheat.

I began to see the opposing sides of everything and the meaninglessness of earthly ambitions. I saw the plausibility of failure being success, and success being failure. I despise success and fear it as much as I wanted it.

My predictions came to pass one after another. Thoughts surfaced in my mind before the public even talked about them. My ideas were adopted or became contentious talking points. Some words and phrases I used became common usage but were never attributed to me. In fact, it practically could not be proved those ideas were from me. To even suggest it would be extremely embarrassing and socially suicidal. The more I succeed, the more I lose.

Although it was impossible to catch up on Additional Mathematics during Pre-University, I realised I was catching up on other subjects and wouldn't fail my examinations. But I wanted to fail, and I didn't study even just before the examinations. It wasn't easy to fail as I found out I was still able to answer those questions. I had to do the only thing left – I submitted blank papers.

When I was conscripted, I decided to rebel against it. Claiming to have lost concentration, I went against nature to appear dysfunctional. Sometimes, ordered to turn left, I knowingly turned right. During lessons and trainings, I adamantly indulged in my own thinking. I consoled myself by planning AWOL, getting thrown into prison, and becoming a monk after my Run Out Date.

I remember the officer who counselled me, saying I had too many "ifs" and "maybes", and that I had to believe in something. It could be anything. Yet from the beginning, it was clear whatever he said, had always been to get me involved in the training and to be positive over it. It was the same unoriginal stuff I heard so often. He was preaching, and his god was the state which gave him bread and butter.

I knew he was right only in the conventional way. I also knew I was "wasting" the most important period of my life and courting disaster. I was quite sure what I wanted to do only in the Army would continue inexorably into civilian life. Yet, like my pursuit of "failure" during Pre-University, I never doubted there was nothing else I should do.

***

I push my chair back and stand up. I'm going to brush my teeth in the toilet, but my body has become soft like melting butter. It spreads on the irresistible bed as my consciousness fades and blends into the emptiness.

Chapter 7
A Meeting of Minds

I was free of worldly concerns. We checked into the same dreary Tokyo hotel we stayed on our way to Los Angeles. We were on the way home this time. How uplifting it was! I was all alone. There was a sense of plenty. But I also felt that for four plentiful days, I would be wallowing like a pig in muck.

Time flies! I've not done any sightseeing nor have I bought popular Japanese foods for loved ones at home. I've not done or achieved anything by any human measure. Before I slept last night, I had the same sickening feeling that in less than two days, I would have to fly home to face the world.

We finish our lunch and walk back to the hotel in the cold.

***

There is nobody else in the small, heated crew room. People in this city live in tiny expensive homes. I'm glad Feng had called me. We sit opposite each other at a table covered with a green cloth filled with cigarette holes and coffee stains. A box of worn mahjong tiles lies on the centre while at one corner sits an empty ashtray.

I say, "After meal service, you spoke to Connie at the back of the cabin. Her almond-shaped eyes were intense. Before that, I saw you with Howard."

He looks at me thoughtfully. "I told her to forget him. She asked why. Yet, she was prepared for what I was going to say. She loves him, but she is sensible. She knows his ways with women, so I didn't tell her about the girl with him. I said he has many admirers, and she is just a friend. She accepted. I suggested she leave him. She said she will do her best."

"I saw you talking to Howard when the rest of us were sleeping on the bus."

"We were in the first row so you guys couldn't hear. He is deep in love. He admitted he went too far to win that girl. I advised him to make a clean break with Connie. I said Connie is a nice girl, and he shouldn't destroy her future. He promised to do it. I told him to tell the other girl he is a steward, not a businessman. He promised to try his best. He said it would be very difficult to do. I understood. I said I will help him get through it."

I get up and make two cups of hot green tea.

Feng continues. "He spent all his money on the girl. He is determined to pay up his debt, and he will. If he keeps away from that girl; even if he doesn't get back his money, he could settle his debts within three years. Easily, with his pay! The problem is the girl. Can he come clean with her? Don't know how she will react. She is very glamorous and has powerful friends."

I place his tea, in front of him, on the table. I lift my handleless cup to my mouth and scrutinise my mind. "You better not get involved. This is very difficult and may be dangerous."

He doesn't pause to think. "Anyone who asks me for help, I have to help."

"You don't have to. Nobody helped you when our colleagues came after you."

"It doesn't matter if no one cares about me. What matters is I care. Everyone is entitled to happiness. I care for what is right, and I care for justice. Everything has to come together in me. I always tell myself to be humble. My enemies can kick me like a dog, insult me and push me into a corner, but I will still do what has to be done. This dog with its back against the wall and head and tail down, will recoil and bite when the time is ripe."

"Not when too much time is involved. Not when you're busy. Not if you get yourself into danger, and the person who needs help is unimportant. I agree when you care for your family. But you can't worry about everybody. You've a duty. If you don't care for yourself, who will? Take care of yourself for the sake of your close ones."

"Some people are more important to me than others. But everyone is important. All are equal. I love all people. People make life meaningful. Love makes life meaningful."

His words nudge me. "Why should we insist on having meaning in life? Our intellect always wants to be clever. It's condemned to look for answers. We dig a hole to see the bottom. We keep digging when we can't find the bottom. Life is life. There is no meaning in it, though you can't say there is no meaning either. It is. Love is love too. Love is beautiful. But how does it make life meaningful? How does loving people make life meaningful?"

"It gives me great satisfaction."

I look at the object, its hand on the table. It exists in a balance of receptivity and aggression. Relaxed, it's ready to make a move.

"I wish I were like you. But it doesn't mean you are right!"

"Remember Ali? After that flight, I got a complaint. He had written me in. The Manager kept siding him, so I walked into the Director's office.

"I told Mr Lee that Ali is a one-way street. I said he doesn't listen to subordinates. He doesn't understand them. He wants them to follow him blindly. He doesn't care when they are hungry or unhappy. It is like he is head of a family. The crew lives thirty thousand feet in the air while management works in the office – on ground. He is that bridge between the management and the crew. But he uses rules to terrorise the crew. He is a warlord who only knows how to take. He demands respect and service. He has no humanity. When crew members see him, they can't function. When they hear he is the purser for their flight, they report sick. How can the crew do well with him around?

"Mr Lee promised to look into it. He has a MBA. He understands all this which I learnt through reading management books."

Feng carries an aura of certainty, with no trace of arrogance. I let myself be carried along: "People like Ali are paid for sleeping and eating while others work. They pay him for doing wrongs. Management is stupid, or knows what it's doing."

Feng looks me in the eye, as though he found a chink in my armour. "That's why we fight for justice. After the complaint, Ali's friends hounded me on my flights. But who cares! The more I am persecuted, the tougher I become."

"Why didn't you go to the union?"

He snaps in irritation. "I couldn't work with the shop stewards. That was why I left the union. I want progress in the Company, in society, but the union is a clumsy elephant. Those unionists sit on their backsides. Many are there to protect their own backsides."

I look at him with admiration. But with sadness, I say, "The unions were crushed. They're now run by 'three-legged' jokers. During elections, jokers appeared and were allowed to be glib. After that, they are like you and me. The difference is they get to hobnob with the bosses. They've two different bosses who kowtow to the same big boss. I don't care who wins elections. Once in power, they are the same animal.

"I did a flight with Ramesh when he was very nice. During briefing, he asked us to vote for the opposition. That was when I understood. Election campaigns were in progress. He told us 'to stop "two-headed" people' (his own words), who look like him from controlling the union. He said they go to the office during days off to make coffee and tea. I wasn't sure he was deliberately making a fool of himself or he was sarcastic. At first, I had difficulty believing he was working for the union. Throughout the flight, he was smiling at the hostesses and slapping stewards on their backs. He said anyone who needed help should just let him know.

"If you find meaning doing good and right, why are those people so different?"

"I don't know why! I don't care! But I want to defeat evil. I only want to bring people to my side. Once they do good, they are on my side."

I try not to think about how I'm performing, since I would lose focus. "You seem to know what is good and bad. If what you think is bad, somehow, is seen as good one day, would you still find meaning fighting them?"

"Never talk about things which didn't happen."

"But it could shed some light on the truth!"

"I don't know the answer, but again it doesn't matter to me. I am a simple man. Once people do good, the past is forgiven. Then the best man wins a job."

Ideas usually jumped at me from all directions during a meeting and led me astray. Then the tendency was for me to lead a discussion astray. I'm not sure this has happened again, but it still seems all right and natural.

I say, "People try to outdo each other all the time. When there is shortage of resources, they do so. When everyone is provided for, they do so. They seek more for themselves and can't stop. They seek advantages in the games called life and the afterlife. When they perceive a large gap between themselves and rivals, and they're lagging, they do things people don't usually do to close the gap. Ramesh says some crew members 'carry balls' to get promoted. I'm very sure he is very good at it; otherwise, why was his promotion so fast?

"People play by rules when they are advantaged by them. Or they are comfortable and don't want to take the risk of breaking those rules. The airline serves free alcohol, against IATA's ruling, to attract passengers. A renowned Frenchman designed the beautiful but impractical *kebaya* which not so subtly exposes hostesses' parts to lonesome, inebriated males. The crews work under unsafe circumstances to complete elaborate services. Aircraft take off and land during heavy thunderstorms to be on time. Is the airline playing foul or looking after passengers and crews? If you benefit from its success, you think they care; if you lose, you say they're dirty.

"Established airlines act aboveboard. Sometimes, they themselves helped set the rules. They stay ahead when everyone follows rules which are difficult for underdogs. Rich countries preach principles and values to keep out competitors after getting to where they are. Then they talk about science, religion and philosophy. They ask what has their bad past to do with the present. Should you win playing by the rules, they would find something else to keep you down; or they shift the goal further away. The intention of human beings is the same when they act high class."

"That is true. Some people are disadvantaged."

"It's an opinion. There are people who spy and work for authorities. Subgroups are tempted to play this game if they aren't fighting their bosses. People like Ramesh rise through the ranks of big entities and prosper because the bosses use them to manage others. In fact, Ramesh is like a mercenary of British India. But these people aren't more sinful than us. We're guilty of sins too which could be of a different nature. The main difference is we are not in their shoes. Different cultures produce different sorts of behaviour. Cultures themselves are influenced by environment and circumstances. If you grew up with Ramesh, it's practically impossible not to be moulded by the culture he was immersed in. If Ramesh is air-dropped into our environment, he will in a matter of time be like us."

***

I feel a tinge of happiness to have been focused on the surface. I know the thing is trying not just to destroy it but to seize me. I notice a pain spreading in my bladder, pressing for attention, and walk to the toilet.

In the constricted space, I stumble over the floor cloth. I find peace. Then I worry I've to return to the room soon. Unzipping my fly, I release a stream. I listen to its sounds, falling on water, to block out thoughts which would bring the thing.

I did very well because our discussion concerned truth and life. They are one of the highest topics to discuss. As the threads wobble in droplets, the seeds of distraction grow like a disease. I realise I was keen to glean something from the discussion because it wasn't mundane gossip, or how to kiss passengers' arses and give whatever they want. All the same, I worry once I'm aware of it, I would be trapped by it and have to think. Then I fumble in what I do. I would ask if I should do the opposite? Or go for something in between – or something else could tear my mind. Once this cycle begins, it gets increasingly difficult to dislodge the thing. I must nip it in the bud. But trying gives it strength.

I should move on, not think about it. I tag on the subject I was avoiding. My imagination makes a picture of the figure in the room, eyelids drooping in reflection. Unrelated thoughts are pushed aside as my mind uses the image to focus. I don't know what to do, but I'm ready for another good fight.

I already zipped up my fly. Gingerly, I push open the door and enter the room. I push aside irrelevant thoughts swarming into my head, again and again, unsure what they are. I direct my attention again at Feng, thinking I should examine what those thoughts were. I know distractions are endless if I allow myself to follow them, except there is a remote chance I'm wrong.

***

The blurry figure, slouched on the chair, is ready to respond.

He sits up. "How can Ramesh be a Purser? At least in Ali's case, it is an oversight of management. Life is not fair. We must fight." As usual, he pronounces words carefully and pauses to string sentences grammatically. It's like he is eating words floating out of his strong and clear mind. A steady hand holds the cup to his mouth. "But Ramesh speaks very well. Both his brothers are famous lawyers. They are good in English."

The word, "English", jolts me.

I tell him, "Lives are tied to human decisions. A step in one direction has consequences coursing down history. Be it technology, beliefs or culture, it starts with one step, leads to another and then another. Each step is linked to the previous one, and unless a concerted effort is made, there can be no change. Have we not used English as the working language, Ramesh wouldn't be pushing his weight around. The use of English is unfair."

His eyelids lift slightly before lowering, and his eyes focus on mine. His lips open in surprise at the fresh idea. "One can't have everything. Sometimes, it is better to make a sacrifice. We have to speak English with other races, especially at work, though we value our language and culture. Use our language at home, so we'll never lose it."

Our discussion has taken a new twist. But I'm doing well, and I've practically kept out the thing.

I say, "We're force-fed a lie for decades. Who continue to use a language at home when it's hardly practised in public? What's the purpose of keeping traditional cultures and values when Western ones are glamorised and instilled in us through the widespread use of English."

As his eyes lose some light, I press on, unwilling to lose momentum. I ignore peripheral distractions and the vague thoughts still slipping occasionally into my mind. "Seventy-five and fifteen percent of the population actually value their languages and cultures since they are the two majorities whose statuses deserve better recognition."

The invisible screen in front of my eyes becomes translucent and my mind less fluid. It worries me the tighter sensation may mean I'm losing focus and freedom. I push aside the thought.

"How long will believers hold out?

"The two percent and the seven percent naturally focus on improving useful English skills as they sacrifice nothing doing so. In fact, the death of vernacular languages suits them since theirs are never relevant. That is why they identify easily with national objectives.

"We say those who are effectively bilingual win, materially and culturally, but reward largely the ones who focus on English and thus speak it better. Is it the marketplace, as claimed, when a powerful hand is manipulating it? The day will come when one is told it's rude not to speak English in public.

"Despite promises, politicians betray you once the wind slows. They've to be pressured all the time. Opponents eat you up bit by bit, if they hadn't done in one gulp. It is either duplicity or a blunder when people are told to keep traditions and choose the language to educate their children in, when English is being made the only practical language at the same time."

The shine in Feng's eyes returns completely as he stands. "The intense seventy-five percent will never lose by the use of English. We're doing well."

I prefer to hear him speaking Hokkien! It always flows from his lips effortlessly. I've no doubt Mandarin would be suitable for him. Were it the working language, Feng would probably have already been a very successful man!

"We're English educated. We experience a big advantage over less-English or non-English users, but lose out to people who focus on English. Yet they insist there is a level playing-field for the different races.

"English (there are three other official languages), is more different from Chinese languages and culture, than the language of any other group in the island. The English educated feel pampered as they only compare themselves with people they are related to. They won't admit their weakness against the minorities and Westerners. The majority are rendered inept, and appear inferior in any interaction with the advantaged – since language (especially when it's spoken) and culture in people are nurtured through generations of conditioning. This competition is set to expand.

"And it isn't just two percent and English-speaking foreigners who are advantaged, as we are led to believe. Another seven percent (through their forebears) have a long association with the English language and British protocol, and Western culture – which were historically well established in South Asia. Ramesh's parents and relatives were sepoys and admin clerks in British India. (I'm excluding the fifteen percent as they aren't competitive.)

"The disparity is worsened by the fact a bigger percentage of the majority is non-English users compared to the other races.

"The English educated then rationalise their failure, to empathise with the plight of their own and to address their own difficulty, with reasons from others."

Feng is adjusting to my uncharacteristic assertiveness. He compresses his lips, pushing them up slightly to one side, as he thinks.

I know I've been eloquent. "It's untrue sociability is less important than money and career. Many of the disadvantaged are successful despite the daunting cultural and language hurdles. They overcame adversities and grew stronger so that the case is now made the government favours them.

Their success distracts us from the fact that despite their contributions, they are social cripples outside normal circles of family and friends because the paramount language of communication and administration in the island is English. English elevates an already glamorised Western culture which the seventy-five percent, whether they are English educated, Chinese educated or non-educated, are not so comfortable in.

"They work harder to achieve an outcome. That is why most of the underclass in this island comes from this group as well. Some taxi drivers and dish washers should have retired. Many of the seventy-five percent and fifteen percent end up with unwanted jobs, or do petty businesses which bring little income and no benefits. People from the seventy-five percent take their own lives when they can't cope since they are practically left out of government assistance – unlike the fifteen percent."

It is hard to convince someone as headstrong and confident as Feng. He won't change his mind unless something happens which shakes him to the core. His view is backed by orthodox thinkers and buttressed by the deliberately cultivated association of heresy with the contrary view. He is prepared to sacrifice himself on the altar of nationalism because of this belief. Nationalism is the sibling of humanism for Feng.

Standing up, he says in a steady voice, "We are a multiracial society. English was chosen because any other language would cause communal strife."

I'm in no mood to back down. He has spouted yet another official view. We've veered from the subject of Ramesh and humanity, to touch on politics and the lives of people. But this is a related subject, one which I am more passionate about.

"They have strengthened the case of people who refuse to speak a language because of race. It's their intention, all along, to promote this view, so they can claim only a foreign language used by two percent can ensure harmony. If seventy-five percent is too small for their language to be the lingua franca, how many percent is?"

I realise I'm holding onto a topic at last. "I'm speaking up because someone has to. I don't expect outsiders to do it. They have to be reminded it's the majority who has, overall, sacrificed. Otherwise, the loud beneficiaries will keep saying they're bullied to further their agenda. I'm answering government critics too. The government won't talk because we are too quiet ever since our leaders were silenced.

"My modest hope is people can continue to live in the multilingual and multicultural environment promised. I've no interest in taking sides because no one deserves more than another. Siding is like love. You soon find out it makes you do rather foolish things for undeserving people.

"Yet we must think for ourselves. How can there be justice when they don't know we are cheated?"

He looks at me with penetrating eyes. "Are you sure you are not being emotional?"

"Not even a book can say everything. Use your imagination to fill the gaps. I'm not learned, but I've trained myself to recognise truth." I feel worried I could have sounded arrogant to Feng.

He sits and squeezes his fist on the table.

"I read the man's speeches; I follow his life. I try to be like him. He is a world-class statesman."

I say, "His policies make us lose two generations before we can say we've narrowed the disadvantaged gap. After that, it won't be so bad when the gap attenuates."

"OK," he sneers for the first time. "Do you have a solution? Remember, we're immigrants with intractable problems. We have nothing besides ourselves. If not for English, there would be famine. We are lucky to have a world class leader with vision and principles."

"You admire both Howard and the man."

"They are good people. Of course, this man is greater than Howard. But it's the heart that matters. If you are lesser, doing small things is enough. To me, everyone has a chance in this world. That's why life is so meaningful."

It is hard to convince Feng, but he's easy to talk to. One of his ideals is an open mind.

"Both men live for themselves. One is more capable. But capability is relative, as you suggested. If you compare that man with more capable people in the world, he is really another Howard."

He doesn't challenge my position this time, so I answer his earlier question. "If four official languages cause much confusion, why can't two come from the people? Mandarin and Malay are more natural. Malay can't replace Mandarin whereas English is destroying both of them. Making English the paramount language makes Malay and Mandarin supporters suspicious of each other whenever either language is used. Malays would not accept a considerable rise of Mandarin when English has been promoted over their language.

"English should be merely a language of interest since it is useful and foreign. It doesn't have to be the first language because we want to learn from the Anglosphere and trade with it. This island shouldn't stick out like a prostitute in Asia."

I am swept along by the surge of thoughts inside my head. Filled with an insecure pleasure, I continue. "Japan is an economic superpower. Taiwan, Hong Kong and South Korea are doing well. The problems some of them faced were bigger than ours. They have natural disasters and large populations to feed. They don't have a strategic harbour like we have. They have little natural resources except people with genes and a culture like ours. The British forces were leaving us. We've racial riots and labour unrest. They have wars and threats of war. None betrayed their root for economic gain. They produce multinationals; we have government companies and continue to kowtow to MNCs.

"English is not the basis of our survival. It gave an initial edge before ineffectiveness and associated problems set in. Is the general populace really better off because of English? The best-paid workers in the world don't speak English. They get good benefits, and don't feel inferior to English speakers in their own country. The lands with the most non-native English users in the world, South Asia and the Philippines, are failures. English is addictive and induces dependence. Smug workers use

English. We structure our economy to make full use of this drug, which we should wean ourselves off.

"What are we telling the young when we cut off communication with the very people we come from for pragmatic gain? One day, they've to lie English is their mother tongue to avoid embarrassment and guilt. This national betrayal is the root of more misguided policies in future. The insidious influence on morals sneaks beyond the tiny island and the present generation, to the dismay of principled people.

"Do the rich stay wealthy forever? Do you think foreigners don't speak better English and won't take your jobs in future, because you speak the language?"

Feng's wide mouth broadens when he smiles. "Some say the seventy-five percent themselves have no common mother tongue." There is no malice on his kind and composed face. He regains my respect. He is equanimous in debate as long as his opponent is sincere.

I've been waiting for this point, anyway. They invented all kinds of reasons to kill Mandarin. "There are many dialects, but one written language and an agreement by Chinese communities throughout the world that Mandarin is their common language. Nantah teaches in Mandarin before the man took down the private university. When it was being built, rich and poor from all the dialect groups donated money. Mandarin is linked to dialects whereas English is linked to the West. Mandarin and dialects support each other and promote Chinese culture. English minimises

Chinese culture and disrupts Mandarin and dialects. You can say Mandarin is the mother of Chinese dialects whereas English is the step language of the people."

He insists. "It is fair to say there is an even playing field for all with English. We believe in meritocracy. It works."

I say, "Every other country understands language is not just a tool for communication. Language promotes its own culture and takes sides. Don't underestimate its underlying agenda. It determines who gets what, and who marries whom.

"The English media are unduly influenced by professionals from the minorities and Westerners. The voices of the seventy-five percent and fifteen percent are drowned. Can the government monitor the media all the time? The media slip in their own agenda at every chance. Capable men are ignored. The drain of wealth and talent from the seventy-five percent through reverse assimilation is covered up with the red herring that Indian girls are losing their prime men. Western mores and English make most people inferior to the two percent and foreigners from the Anglosphere. They make us into toothless, inelegant machines of wealth whose minds are seduced or pushed around by smooth talkers.

"It is natural to allow majorities some advantage through the support of their languages so that they can be generous to minorities without being overwhelmed. Yet there are laws to ensure minorities are at least equally represented in public institutions, but never the other way round. If the government is sincere about levelling the playing field, why are they ignoring the disadvantages faced by the majority?"

"What other disadvantages are faced by the majority?" Feng seems genuinely interested. He is encouraging me with his openness.

"Society's views are moulded by years of colonialism, Western domination – and now, social engineering. When I was young, we admire the looks of Alan Tang and Lin Ching Hsia and aspire to speak and carry ourselves like them. Today, this is unfashionable (with derogatory names like *cheena*, becoming part of the local vocabulary) while intermarriages and Western norms are subtly and consistently glamorised by the media. Unlike the days of colonialism, you don't suspect being manipulated."

"Are you saying Ramesh is very advantaged?"

"He plays the victim because people tend to think racial minorities are poorly treated. The fact is in this island, overall, English gives minorities a powerful leverage. The two percent and Westerners are kings because of an additional leverage: culture. The glaring symptoms are everywhere, but you've to swallow your false pride to see them. This island is always different from other countries, yet using narrow arguments, the minorities are accusing the majority and the government of discrimination. They never say they themselves are openly discriminatory in opposing any form of influence by the majority, whereas Westernisation is zealously embraced."

"We will become one people." His face is glowing and positive again. He has resilience. It comes from his love of people.

"But the majority is assimilated by the smaller groups (it should be the other way), while their cream is constantly lured away by Western countries. Their beliefs and pride are systematically destroyed by the very person who lamented there is nothing to "hold them back" when mandatory conversion is even practised by some.

"We created a mixed pot of people whose roots float on water. Like the country, they are *kiasu,* afraid to lose out and jousting for advantages. That's the real glue which holds them temporarily together. It's the main reason we have the highest emigration rate per capital in the world. The discrimination and other policies unintentionally produce a birth rate in which the highly stressed pool keeps diminishing while that of the laid-back welfare recipients keeps increasing.

"We will be hollowed out quickly and need constant replenishment, but the use of English puts the very people needed in a very troublesome situation. The cycle of unequal treatment will be repeated. The new immigrants will suffer as the institutionalised squeeze on the majority continues.

"We should encourage immigration in earnest, as he is old. He has done much for himself, and is the only person in a position to address this issue, but we are waiting. He kills our souls, so it's very difficult now he couldn't bring back those values. Immigration must be carefully planned, and would be tough to manage in a sudden influx."

I'm happy with my performance. Standing, I walk once more to the toilet. I've wanted to do this for some time. I see myself in the mirror and instantly look away. Maybe, I shouldn't have done that. I keep thoughts away though that was what I came to the toilet for.

I step back into the room. The window curtain is drawn aside. Outside, the sky is grey with streaks of red and gold. Feng is seated on his chair. He is not a blurry figure, and the lighted room and everything in it, is as clear as the skies after heavy rain. Even the Japanese women having afternoon tea below, and their giggles, feel like clearly drawn lines in this place bathed in soft light. Spanking clean overcoats and thick jackets would be hanging from a rack or lying on empty chairs.

Feng's voice comes out clearly. It stops and moves carefully like a sputtering train. "He's a great man. He wants us to be loyal to our country but never forget where we come from."

I am aware I say with much clarity and lightness. "He knows how small the nation is. People like Ramesh want us to forget our roots, despite trying to settle in the West, because they thrive on our disunity. English creates an artificial divide within the seventy-five percent, even beyond this island, for the benefit of some. It is also very important to the man when any other language would hobble him. That's also why Ramesh demands his subordinates speak only English.

"Some claim the man is playing racial politics, when he says it's silly to lose an identity nurtured over five thousand years, encompassing one-and-a-half billion people worldwide at present. But he is right and is admitting past excesses. Why replace it with a new tag of two million, which couldn't last another one-hundred-and-fifty years? The Speak Mandarin Campaign, SAP schools and so on are compensation for not recognising the proper status of Mandarin. Mandarin doesn't destroy dialects as some imply, to cause dissension against it. It's English which is killing all local languages and dialects. Mandarin makes way for English to prevail, but they now say Mandarin is unfair.

"They show ugly faces when they hear Mandarin or dialects spoken nearby. They complain when a single member of the service staff couldn't speak English. As they decry being marginalised and discriminated against, they ignore the pains suffered by the real victims of language and cultural oppression who are silent for a long time. Why even accept a little inconvenience, when an inch could lead to a yard? How can they let the discriminated heave a sigh of relief at a slight improvement of circumstances? It would be disastrous if the relief brings a smile. They no longer appreciate English is allowed its pivotal role in so far as the other three official languages are not stifled. Nobody stops someone from taking up Mandarin if the person wants to.

"I won't compress my identity into a tiny convenience store. I will always be linked to my wider identity. I am linked to the island, the Chinese people, the human race and the world."

Feng says, "Aren't these concepts contradictory? Which is more important to you: being a Chinese or being a citizen of this nation? Not that I am against your idea, I am only thinking."

"You don't ask whether the human race or the world is more important because you belong to both. Can you say your beliefs are less important than your country or vice versa?"

"I treasure my identity …" Feng is talking, but I don't know what he is saying. My concentration is wavering. This is due to my realisation, a while ago, I had clarity. Something has been nagging me since.

I begin to think how my face differs from his as the object in front changes one expression after another. Now, there are two faint lines on his laughing cheeks, and then his lips separate to reveal partially a white row with gaps. The brow between his eyes crinkles. I wish I had a face like his. He doesn't worry about it, and lets others do the thinking. He doesn't even let them, he only lives. My head jerks left and right, to dislodge the thoughts still coming at me, quickly enough so he wouldn't see what I'm doing.

As my state of mind returns to the previous groove, I hear him instantly: at first a little vaguely. "This island is developing its own culture. Soon the Chinese here will have nothing in common with those in China: only differences. Then some people cut down the bridge that links." There is sadness in his voice.

I gather my mind. "They're Sinophobes, and Chinese who can't understand identity doesn't confer material benefits on one party all the time. Timing isn't a privilege. Politics is a tool by which one manipulates another for own ends. Everyone is a politician. Some say what they want and some believe what they want. What they do depends on time and circumstances. The favourite lie is to use half-truths as truth."

"It is important we are interested in politics. You can't escape from it," he says with self-assurance.

"There are marked differences even in this tiny island, between a Chinese person living in the main shopping district and another in a government flat in the suburbs. They are shaped by different environments and experiences. Similarly, a Chinese living in Beijing is different from his brother in Shanghai, or his cousin in a small village in Fuqing, and will of course be different from his sister living in this island. He will also be different from his son who lives in the same apartment as him, since they're from different generations.

"Yet, beneath outward differences, all of them share characteristics shaped by millennia of conditioning. The way one thinks and feels won't go easily, whether the person likes it or not. There are ingrained habits like thrift or parsimony, hard work or aggression, scholarship or studiousness, sense of shame or consciousness of face, gambling or risk taking, and so on. Chinese people are generally good in maths but clumsy with Western customs. They've unique physical characteristics which can be healthy or unhealthy. People see their reflections in the very faces in front, and if they don't like them, they will cringe to learn truth takes no sides.

"That's why when they recognise their own ugly side, but don't understand the world enough, they despise each other. You thought they would use their lopsided familiarity of close ones to understand them, but you're wrong. They hate one another when they want something from a limited pie. After all, they've learnt it is politically correct to distance themselves from their foreign siblings. But it depends on how the brothers and sisters fare in the material world when people pick and choose. This tendency, they wouldn't admit, is a shame. Not everyone is like you, full of humanity and love.

"Often, people act with hypocrisy and pretences; and if they claim not to be something, it doesn't change them."

I can see his strong face with prominent cheekbones clearly. He isn't affected by my compliment, though I notice a momentary glimmer in his intelligent eyes. This should be the way a person lives. There is no self-fixation. Everything is done naturally. The tanned skin on his exposed areas is tough and moist, like strong leather. The lines on his forehead fade, though I still see tiny wrinkles at the corners of those glinting eyes and the cracked edges of his slightly slanted mouth. I'm reminded of someone.

"We do our part. That's all we can do," he says. It's not bad to hear this. There is hope. Someone hasn't lost the human values of dignity and loyalty. Feng's words cheer, except I know we are fighting a losing battle.

I continue to push myself. I'm not going to fail after going this far. "China has huge potential. The people are able and intense. It has pent up energy. Now it's reforming its system, its economy will probably grow very fast. When their income levels catch up with other countries', outward differences with us will be smoothed over.

"Modern technology will be used to accentuate differences. There will be quarrels in the short term when some don't like the right of others to prosper, especially, if the others were previously poor. Sadly, China is the only hope for the revival of Mandarin in the island."

"Sometimes, I write to him. Twice he wrote back." Feng is peering into my brain again. "He admitted this is an unlikely place to form a nation."

"He builds a corporation. Nothing is as important as profit. People are taught to hate anything that can lower the price of their assets. Some are very rich, some rather poor. The worst is squeezed in between. Most are stressed and overworked. Productivity and value-add are obsessions. Talent and hard work are valued traits. People check the price of everything. Values have to be taught because there is a price for everything. People feel good to think they use English. They've grafted butts onto Asian faces and become Jacks-of-languages-and-cultures, masters of none. Solution from experts: further grafting.

"I appreciate the stability he brings. But this place is too small to be governed by an ambitious man of that calibre. That's why his hand is everywhere in the island, yet he is busily gathering praise outside it. His experience is keenly exported to larger countries looking for solutions to ancient problems. Like a company selling successful ideas tested in tiny projects – except it asks for no fees.

"It's unlikely he and his team could have ruled a large state or even done it well. But he is the real chairman of our airline. Without his attention and support, it wouldn't be what it is today.

"The people are starting to hate the man who moulded them, but they'll always think highly of themselves. He told them they threw away enough, except the creation no longer believe its creator."

I find myself asking: Why am I worrying about people who are anathema? Why should I care for people who are to be turned into anathema? Didn't the prevailing anathema come from people? Why bother when what is anathema comes and goes? And who knows what the world will become, because anything can happen!

Perhaps loyalty is getting redundant. But those hurling the rocks want to live in its glass houses.

Feng lowers his purposeful gaze, revealing double eye lines below straight black hair. He looks like the Hokkien orator who should have been PM, the man whose high standards have to be emulated by PM, the man really instrumental for the independence of this country.

Even as layers of stories are made about one whose underlings are praised and excessively rewarded, the truth about the other lies twisted and buried in the deep recesses of history.

All I've done is keep the thing out of my mind. Yet I know, sometimes, it's impossible to do so. As Feng stands and stretches his arms, his hands seem to slide over the surface of my body, making me jump out of my skin.

***

"You want more tea? Green tea is good." His solid voice trips and restarts. The words skim my eardrums as I look at his clear hands holding a cup each, and he walks to the counter. Everything is so clear I don't care to breathe. I haven't finished what I've in mind to say, but I'm no longer interested. My attention can't leave this new awareness.

"I've to go." I put on my overcoat and open the door. I'm so light as I stride on the soft carpet to the waiting lift. *What is this? And why?* I dare not think about it, and I daren't tell myself not to think about it.

My stomach feels empty. I see clearly I've to fill it, yet it doesn't really matter. The lift opens with a soft clunk: so clear it's loud in my ears.

In a flash, I know what I believed in is true. The discussion with Feng is red herrings that came out of ordinary existence: full of fury, but meaningless in the true world!

I walk quickly in the cold night, in and out among people, on pavements lighted by street lamps. Sometimes, I break into a run as I look out for a suitable restaurant.

Chapter 8
A Taste of Freedom

Calm down, I told myself. This wasn't the first time freedom came. Wrapped in my overcoat, I felt comfortable and secure. A pleasant cold brushed gently the sides of my face. I didn't have to walk fast to generate heat, so I slowed my pace. I recognised the street. Soon I would reach Tokyo station.

It wasn't a normal feeling. The thing was gone. I was almost frightened when discrimination suddenly disappeared. Shapes were still there, but the lines had disappeared. I couldn't make out those divisions I used to see, smell, hear or cognise. Blobs of nakedness: a solid mass here, a less solid one there; a transparent mass here which I walked through, a translucent blob there: floated everywhere, and made up the undifferentiated mass. Everywhere was filled with nakedness.

Something luminous floated forward with a jerk. It was rather weightless, almost like a little pressure. Conscious of thoughts and feelings (emotionally and physically); it walked, looked, smelled, heard and imagined. A vague point with an organ in which thoughts sprouted into invisible lines, long and short, and then died, and feelings that stuck to them like flesh, died with them. A desperate thought with a unique character clung at its edge like a street urchin. No pity for it, no "self-pity" as it tried to dress me up. After that, more fake covering for me to accept: more uncomfortable existence. Seductive! Seditious would be a better word.

I understood those ideas showing in my head but couldn't find fitting words for them. I said, "Objects, sounds." Those abstract words clung to my tongue and wouldn't let go. Vertical shapes vaulting on stiff legs, emitting primeval sounds. Two shafts squirming inside pliable tubes, clenched digits peeking out. I couldn't call them "arms" and "fists" anymore. Arms and hands used to carry trays for passengers while digits became rocks to emphasise a point. Functionality lost its meaning that night.

Lighted buildings with antennae towered over on both sides, like giants peering at miniscule ants. Their foundations plunged deep into the ground like dental roots. Matter was taken bit by bit from another existent, before, then piled atop each other. If those roots decayed, the building would topple over this nakedness to make one!

Within these hollow structures that night, games played out routinely brought mundane glory and routine destruction. Existents felt, wrote on tables, and exchanged emotional words. They sucked external existents into ravenous bodies before releasing them into half-clogged pipes. These substances then entered more pipes and left the buildings. The redundant bodies with muck inside, copulated as fat mice do in sewers, lay on beds like dogs after eating and vomiting, and died inside the buildings like dead insects.

People on the street or peering from high windows didn't notice me. I no longer cared anyway. The inanimate buildings were neutral stuff. By the roadside, they stagnated, round bellies exposed to lingering air, for the food sucked in to slide down and nature calls. Those indifferent blobs could change their minds, open intransigent doors suddenly, and coddle me like precious passengers in the cars!

Caught in the jam, a beautiful blonde in a taxi slumped against the back of the seat behind. The metallic object was ferrying the voluptuous object, its creamy white skin hot and prickly inside winter clothes, to a brothel in Ginza. Feeling her desiccated breasts scrape the well-padded cups, she clapped her silky hands with glee: "Good to cheat men, good to cheat them."

A louse attached a nit to a pubic hair before feasting again, unwittingly, bringing on existence in return for its own. It helped slim long thighs, as cancer cells fed on the good host.

The woman took a book from her handbag to calm her restless mind. She looked at her watch, and emitted a helpless sigh. She thought about causes and effects, and became more afraid and confused. She concentrated on her breaths.

Seen and unseen, everything overlapped and conjoined that night in a monstrous web. Different things were equal and same, expansive and infinite, primal and elegant; cruel and kind, horrible yet consoling at the same time. Existence encompassed blobs of mess: rolling by faster than my legs could walk, floating by as naked as I was. Their nakedness brushed against mine, not touching, as their "breaths" – not warm, cold or lukewarm – soothed. They weren't me, I wasn't them; we were each other, part of the same existence.

Sounds snarled their way into my ear canals, twirling like cotton buds. Sashaying melodies from a building stroked my once troubled heart. Exhaust smells, naked like newborn babes, drifted up and gathered within my nose, before filling my brain. Headlights detoured round me as the roads crawled between the naked buildings, and slithered below spaces crowded with the traffic. And the pavement slipped beneath my feet to shelter the earth below – with tunnels and caves – for living existents.

I didn't think much. I knew I shouldn't think purposely.

***

I often asked, *why is there existence?* Straightaway, *why should there be inexistence?* had raised its hand. Existence had no straight answer except an innocent tongue sticking out. I realised existence never asks to be born. Nor could it ever asked not to be born. Nobody, nothing ever played a role in its fate. It never needs to be created. It is not witless. Nothing comes before it, nothing after it, and nothing exists outside it – because nothing is also existence. Existence, like sexual love, only needs the right conditions. Then, it appears. There is no being which causes it, though we continue to look for a cause which can empathise.

We create sad stories, only to change them into happy ones. We create hopelessness and injustice, and replace them with the myth of salvation. We yearn for existence when it isn't there, but wish it went away when it's there. But existence comes and goes. It does not care how you feel. Thinking about it doesn't change its intrinsic form. When it goes, you can't call it back. You may only wish it stayed.

You can't ascribe a physical form to inexistence, yet inexistence is also existence. A nonsense idea even if it's false, exists in spite of its lack of substance. It exists despite its apparent inexistence. The idea of one trillion exists but has no form or substance. Smells, pleasant and unpleasant; feelings, happy or sad or angry; touch, hard or soft, hot or cold: are all empty and exist. I've realised inexistence is another form of existence.

Existence is nothing. It is a quality without quantity. That's why physical mass is made of nothing, except adjectives. Even if existence were full of physicality, every physical existent would have the same value as inexistence. Even if there were only physical existence and no inexistence, each existent is as good as nothing. Existence is therefore the same as inexistence. Existence is inexistence, inexistence is existence.

Existence and inexistence are relative. Their intrinsic nature is isness, yet isness is neither existence nor inexistence. Infinity is easily conceived with isness whereas it would be impossible to imagine infinity if the world is something or nothing. Imagine something is infinite: it comes to an end, and you encounter inexistence. Imagine inexistence: you encounter existence.

We look for a causal being to help tackle our problems but encounter isness, because the ultimate Truth never changes or compromises. Isness is not in space and time. It's the central aspect of the threesome (isness, existence and inexistence), the only true absolute unaffected by thoughts. Isness would still be that absolute if there were Creators of Creators.

The taxi was still keeping pace with me in the heavy traffic. The woman's lined eyes shut, brows a delicate knot of concentration, as she tried to forget her self-importance and relax.

In expensive clothes, and her face made up with the best products money could buy, she looked naturally beautiful and exotic. But I had a vision her face was a mask and everything she projected was a lie. Even if she didn't lie, everything would still be a fake. I wanted to touch her warm flesh to prove I was wrong, but she was behind the glass. Even if I could reach her, there would be nothing to touch for she wasn't that woman anymore. All her make-up and clothes had fallen away, and she wasn't the solid object I used to imagine her to be. Even her internal organs were floating.

Floating in what? I stopped walking and held the lamp-post for support. I closed my eyes and tried not to think. But I was imagining words? Words were floating in and about her, and between her, under her; and they were keeping her in place. I saw *female, slim, glamorous, materialistic, young, well-dressed, shapely, sexy, tender, soft*. And more words! They were contending with each other. *Male and female, fat and lean, glorious and pitiful, rich and poor, old and new, classy and cheap, straight and curved, seductive and dull, cruel and caring, hard and soft, long and short ...* I saw words without matter. Like the woman who was merely another word, they were empty. Mere ideas, or adjectives. And those adjectives: empty, isness. I opened my eyes.

She opened hers too and saw me. She looked away. I felt the door. The driver turned around and started. Eyes opened wide. I continued feeling the metal. Felt its coldness, heat within, hardness, smoothness, curve. ... Saw it was black in the dim light. Heard it purr. Smelled intoxicating fumes. Felt the car vibrate, twitch. It moved, leaving gradually. I thought: *adjectives made up the noun which was acted upon by verbs*. A ghostly interconnected mess. The driver's mouth was opened. His eyes were "falling out". Then they were opening and closing quickly. Blinking: that was the word they used. I had to remove my hand. He tried to drive away, but the taxi didn't get far as it was among the crawling vehicles. I thought again. *The noun made up of adjectives tried to drive a noun away: verbed the noun, made up of more adjectives. And the verb got adverbed.* Nothing but words. Words or existence appears out of isness and disappears into isness.

The noun made up of adjectives tried to drive a noun away, carefully. Is the whole world nothing but words? And each word survives and dies as another word emanates. The world of isness has been, is, and will always be the same. Though the word is gone, it never leaves the infinite archive. The archive is a part of isness; it is isness. Before existence is inexistence, isness; and before inexistence is existence, isness. The archive, therefore, never needs to expand.

Those concepts were worth exploring, but I would be driving out this state of mind. I had to choose between dwelling on this revelation and attempting a worldly discovery which would drive out that revelation. I couldn't decide. I stopped thinking. But when I were finally ready to think about the problem, I might forget it was there, I thought. Or I remember the problem but forget what it was about. Or I remember the problem and what it was about, but it's meaningless because I forget something crucial. I couldn't ask someone for a pen to write down the problem by a light so I could read about it later. It was even more difficult when I couldn't speak proper Japanese. Trying to ask would itself almost certainly banish this state of mind. And if I didn't think, I would've denied myself the possibility of any new discovery.

Was there a choice? I had to choose something or risk ending up with nothing. By not exploring, I was already getting nothing. I had to take a risk. Using a thought to make myself give up an idea rather than taking the risk. Both phenomena – taking the risk and the thought of taking the risk – were working together. The thought was making it easy for me to take the risk of not exploring. I could never hold back thoughts and only take the risk, anyway. But who could say with certainty? Maybe it could this time.

Anyway, I regretted not purely letting go again. What was the use of regret? I couldn't escape from its clutch. Was there something absolute about regret? Stop now before it got worse or too late. More unnecessary thoughts instead of action! I could have used this moment to really take a risk this time. All the same, regret was useless. *Concentrate! Release!* Alas, thoughts after thoughts. I repeated: there is no such a thing as letting go thoughts without the intrusion of other thoughts, which are often only trying to help, once you are conscious of your intention. In fact, my best efforts (the pure or the nearly pure ones), had never been noticed, and would never be. These good efforts, if there were any, would never be noticed. … Ah existence after existence! Mere existence.

Thoughts grew, died, grew and stagnated, and a phenomenon was born. The thoughts were the problem which stuck in my mind in the form of words. A problem growing out of individual thoughts became a single phenomenon, and was remembered as such. Not going or going, it would die like the cheesy existence I squeezed out in Los Angeles. Or it could stay on like the building or the taxi; or else link up with other experiences like the complicated woman.

The driver's hostile eyes stared from inside the stationary taxi. It seemed my own eyes were looking at me, so I waved at him lightheartedly. That made his eyes blink furiously again. The woman's eyes were still closed, shutting her off from the outside world. Still she couldn't escape from being a part of me even as in front of this unfettered mess, vehicles and lights floated by slowly. After that were the crawling humans who were also floating, and then a row of bright, green taxis outside the big hole below outstanding Japanese characters and the English words "Tokyo Station". Inside the bright building: more people and existents.

A gap within the traffic opened. Behind the wheel, the driver straightened and drove his vehicle to join the others in front. Other vehicles filled the gap left behind.

***

I came to the deserted path leading to the Palace. The other day, the signs were pointing the way for passersby and tourists, but tonight those rectangles bearing the same words don't have a role. Their previous role was an excuse for their existence that day. Now they sat on the tree trunks, unashamed and unapologetic.

That day, I was annoyed one of the signs was located in a poor position, or else I thought it was excessive. It looked so *wasteful*. It seemed things either outlive themselves, or exist from the beginning as deadwood. At least twenty thousand nuclear bombs were painstakingly made after decades of research involving people and money, but none has been used. Half a billion sperms try their luck in each ejaculation, yet most of the time, none gets accepted. Much time and effort are wasted when diligent people spend entire lifetimes searching, only find the vague answer, if they are "lucky", when they are about to die. And what guarantee is there he will remember that answer, when he needs it, on his deathbed? Or finding what he is looking for, he does all that is necessary and right; and then what? Is he better for it? Yet without waste, nothing could be achieved in this contradictory world. Waste is unavoidable. So when people assure me repeatedly there is purpose in life, I wonder. I understood now why the trees looked uneasy the other day, sapped of confidence, and feeling out of place.

(But situations described by words like "wrong", "excessive", "unnecessary", "wasteful" are relative since in some cases, they weren't negative. The man who sacrifices his people for his own ends is a traitor, but once he makes them think it was in their interest, he isn't seen as one.)

I looked at the trees for the first time since my arrival. A disconcerting consciousness hung over them. The dim light revealed spreading leaves and dark craggy trunks, embracing everything else with their mystic existence. Each of the trees was unique, yet none stood out as different. They were identical and each doesn't need a number to differentiate it from others. They weren't digits which clever humanists tell us not to accept. Big or small, domineering or timid, beautiful or horrible, they were all equal in that commune of trees, signs – and me.

Nothing was a waste. Waste wasn't even conceivable because the kind of thinking leading to it had disappeared. There was no apology for existing – and no discrimination. No thing owed anyone or anything, anything. Hypocrisy is useless. All the trees did was acknowledge each other; my presence and all presence. They didn't even have to do it, and they didn't do it. Their heads were bowed, arms were opened – in respect – to accept. Each was minding its own business, brimming with the existence which altogether filled the entire atmosphere.

A slight cold moved across. Something big landed on the branches above, shook it and went to sit on another tree. Then it flew away. Another rush of wind came and did the same to the first tree. The branches waved and the leaves rustled as the earth held the serpentine roots tightly, squeezing into every corner.

The crisp air coursed through me, when I breathed it in, and filled me with invigorating existence. Freed from thoughts, existence was still revealing itself in its original form. It overflowed from space: from the leaves, the branches and the trunks; from the ground and from the air. Existence uncovered and unsegregated, which I couldn't escape from even if I wanted to. I was inside it, I was it. How could I leave it when I was it? It touched and held me everywhere.

My underwear was caught between my buttocks: existence was touching existence, buried in it, squeezed between blobs of it. They weren't unbearable, as though it didn't matter they were friends or enemies anymore. And I realised it was all about existence encountering existence, while in between were other existences, yet there was simply only one existence.

Fingers, joined to my palms, were happily touching each other. My tongue no longer felt trapped or nauseating, as saliva oozed out easily down the gullet. My head was clear like a mirror. I realised my arms were not tools of servitude. Time stood still, stuck like a headache which wouldn't go away nor get worse or better. Another moment after this one was impossible.

I was usually buffeted by thoughts which pushed me in all directions. This was me, but I couldn't lose those pictures. Why did I wait for the market to fall further when it tanked? I had to keep myself clean not only because it was healthy, but I would look better. I shouldn't stay long under strong sun or my light skin would burn. I shouldn't use sunblock as it caused cancer. Whatever happened to the world would affect me and vice versa.

But now I was free. I owned nothing and cared for nothing. The past and future didn't worry me. Thoughts slid off a raincoat. I was a mere existent. In fact, "mere" was a wrong word because this nakedness was clearly superior to my previous state. I tried to understand why a thought vanishing as a new one appeared was perfectly fine. I didn't know where to begin. I couldn't think, in a world beyond reason, about something.

I lowered myself onto the bench under the dim light, not worried if it was dirty, so long as I didn't notice. It wouldn't be an issue even if it was dirty and I noticed it, anyway.

In the distance, the restaurants were looking at me with smiling eyes. The one I was looking for had a complicit smile on its lips. It was waiting, but I was in no hurry. Maybe I didn't even want to eat. I was drunk with agonising pleasure.

***

What was I thinking of when I left Feng suddenly? I thought it is unfair to say English is the most commonly used language in the world. What was true, however, was that some of the most influential countries with smaller populations spoke English more than any other language in the world. Yet here, with the trees, it was practically useless.

While people in the region where I lived and other parts of the world took pride in their own languages and cultures despite being poor, the little island was praising itself for its realism, as it looked smugly out of the taxi, thinking it has beaten nature.

All of a sudden, the world began to change. I knew it would happen sooner or later. I thought too much, but maybe the thing overstayed somewhere and had to return anyway. Existence in its naked form was withdrawing, not into a hole, but into existence itself. It was hiding, covering its nakedness surely but shyly, as though entering a cold room, the sweat had quickly disappeared. It was hard to believe, not long ago, the same existence had been brash and confident.

And lines like male or female, handsome or pretty, love or hate were getting clearer and clearer. I was conscious of being all alone and helpless. My troubles were reappearing and growing.

The streets were as quiet as a mouse. A few puddles of light from the tops of lamp-posts and once colourful shops opposite, were left. I got up, wiped my overcoat carefully where I had sat on the seat and ran across the empty road. The restaurants were closed. I walked alongside dim buildings with fear. A taxi slowed quietly below the big "Toyko Station" sign. People were gathered around a tricycle covered in ghostly light. Whitish steam plumes rose from the warm vehicle. I was trembling.

I waited with unease. A few Japanese words, some gesticulations and facial expressions between us allowed the man in white to understand. A steaming bowl of soup ramen with two slices of three-layer pork cost four hundred yen. A boiled egg would be good for nutrition. That added, painfully, to five hundred yen, my entire breakfast allowance. At home, I could get two full meals with that money in a "hawker centre". However, the meal was delicious: a relief. But it was due partly to the cold and, of course, the price. I worried the food wasn't enough. I had to go to Lawson nearby, to buy some pastry to eat before checking out.

Quite a lot to go before I reached the warm hotel. All was normal. Crew members were resting for duty in the afternoon. I didn't think I could sleep.

Chapter 9
Disastrous Moments

The black in a white singlet and tight black jeans squats on the side of the uneven cobblestone street, one knee close to the ground. His hand at the end of a muscular arm, methodically presses a button to flick open and close a gleaming switchblade. Boredom sits on his smooth young face as cold eyes peer up, beneath the shelter of a black hat, at me. As I near him, he spews French-sounding words. I can't understand those words.

I'm again alone and bored. The thing has been following me since I stepped out of the hotel in Ferdinand Bolstraat: as I walked along Singel and Leidseplein. It lurked behind me and hid in shadows in front, in the sweltering heat.

I don't understand why I'm doing this. It seems it's one of those onerous habits which formed and grew and became entrenched. These habits grow like beansprouts, become parts of us, and direct and control us with their unthinking tentacles. They free our consciousness, temporarily, from tiresome thoughts, but they also stubbornly refuse to do for us what we need.

More than likely, this habit is a response to the thing. I follow this ritual faithfully nowadays. It's hard to break the ritual even when I want to. Now the thing is ready to seize my brain again and tear me apart. I'm not about to let it do so.

I shake my head at the black man. He realises I don't understand the language he is speaking in.

"Five guilders," he attempts haltingly as he switches to English. He points to my pocket, then his chest. The palm opens in front of me.

I know what to do. I learnt to love living on the edge because it removes me from the thing. The thing batters me, but trains me to take pain. His knife is mundane, a harmless object compared to the thing. I shan't take out my wallet for it to be snatched away. I remember a five guilder note in my pocket. I would only lose a pittance if I let him examine the money and get robbed of it.

His rapacious eyes look at the smooth green note in my hand. He takes it calmly. The knife scrapes it, but he is pretending. The blade barely touches the surface as I watch the crisp note stay in his hand.

I know he is keeping it. I walk in Dam Square in relief: to waste myself in its harsh reality, beside dark canals, past smelly open-air urinals. I gave up guilders to satisfy my sympathy and curiosity, but it's really to win a respite from the thing.

There are windows with pink lights still, in the late morning, as a few lighted up. Some have the curtains drawn apart. Each room with open curtains has a woman sitting on a tall stool or standing by it. Most of the women wear short skirts or bikinis unless they're very fat. Miscreants and degenerates walking by, sidestep dogs' excrement. Tourists chatter excitedly and gape at smiling prostitutes trying to make eye contact with men.

***

People loiter in the still air where a flowery smell lingers. The glass windows in front of my tired legs reveal the bright café is quite empty inside.

I push open the creaky door and sit at a plain four-seater table at the end of the warm room, with my back against the wall. A timid young man with sunken cheeks sits behind the wooden service counter, two tables away on my right. He sucks the shortening cigarette hungrily and stares at the burly waitress with a white face and half-closed eyes.

The middle-aged woman, standing diagonally at the table in front of me, waits in silence for the old man to order. A big chubby hand clutches a writing pad; the other holds a small pencil. The old man couldn't decide, and she sways a little. Her large nose pushes when she yawns like a hippo. The hand with the pencil pats the quivering mouth.

I watch her open mouth with interest. She notices, stops yawning and speaks gruffly across the tables. I can't understand Dutch, but I say loudly: "beer!" Her eyes try to focus. They close and open. The obscene mouth opens and shuts again. It mumbles. Broad heavy legs carry away her body.

I wait for the beer for company. I ruminate. *Is the waitress the thing?* After all, she is waiting. But the thing is in me, and is amorphous and blur.

Near the end of sleep this morning, I had two dreams. I can't remember what they were, but the second continued the first. The first had a problem I didn't manage to solve. I then drifted in an uneasy sleep and entered the second dream where I recalled the problem was unsolved. I continued trying to solve it as I tried to forget in the dream. I drifted out into sleep again, but was increasingly awake as I thought and slept. I realised I was hovering between a dream state and reality, and became very disturbed. I felt strongly the question had to be solved, but I couldn't do it. I didn't even remember what it was about. I was waking and told myself the problem was a mere dream. But I couldn't discard it. Even a dream had to be solved, my other part insisted. There could be meaning in it leading to the ultimate Truth, I thought. I became wide awake and very afraid over what I could have missed.

I could say, eventually, it was a dream, and it should be forgotten. I would probably be right, I told myself. I decided to take a risk and leave the dream. So, a little logic could replace a larger problem. Yet knowing the dreams existed, the vague problem must be solved. I've to recall the forgotten problem in the discarded dreams.

Dreams, sometimes, even continue into four or five episodes. I would ask if reality and the present weren't dreams.

**

The door opens, and an odd couple walks in. There is a ring of familiarity to it. I think: *am I in a dream?* Ramesh, his chocolate face glowing, is holding the hand of a young and beautiful blonde in a white mini-dress. His head is cocked upright in triumph. A wicked grin rests naturally on the girl's face, one men couldn't resist. She is tan and slim, has shapely long legs and is one head taller, even as an Afro-wig sits on his small head. He wears a well-pressed dark suit with a bow tie. A rose boutonniere is pinned on the left lapel.

I look away quickly, before he sees me. To my dismay, they stop at the table in front of the old man. They're debating whether to stay. I'm lucky, for one hand holding a bottle, his other pulls the chair facing me for the girl to sit. Then he walks round the table and sits with his back towards me. The perfume smells like a mix of petrol and insecticide on his body.

The air-conditioning is weak in the simple room even for me in light clothing near the humming apparatus. Ramesh, wet with perspiration, places the dark green bottle I now recognise as a Dom Perignon (introduced recently to the First Class with fanfare) on the table. When he sees the waitress glance at him, he removes folded tissues from his trouser pocket, dabs his face and neck dry, and plants the wet lump on the table. He makes the mistake of snapping his tiny fingers at the waitress.

The slightly damaged label facing me shows the bottle was the one he wanted me to carry for him. When I refused like the first time, he had stormed away. Then he stared at me whenever our paths met on board, but when I looked back with no sign of concern, he would leave.

The waitress's eyelids lifts. She wouldn't look his way. Five minutes later, she comes to me, like a sleepwalker with a glass of gold on a round serving tray. She drops a thick coaster on my table and puts the beer on it. A layer of whitish foam on the liquid overflows the rim down to the table slowly, creating a beautiful sight. I give her two coins, and a third guilder as a tip. The eyes almost close when she collects the coins, and grunts.

The blonde waves sexily. The waitress gets irritated and lumbers to Ramesh. Her nose lifted as she looks curiously at the hair on his head.

The two ladies trade Dutch sentences – the blonde overly charming, the waitress glum and surly. The blonde's antics frustrate women. She points to the wet part of Ramesh's shirt sticking to his chest. The waitress shrugs big shoulders and shuffles to the counter. She stands there and gazes into the street as more agitation gathers her face.

A breath of malevolence hangs in the air. I've to see what is unfolding. I take the adjacent seat (right behind the old man), so Ramesh wouldn't see me if he turns around.

Ramesh produces two triangles and unfolds them into cones. (I saw those paper cups in the Hotel lobby in Tokyo. They were for guests to fill with drinking water.) He gives them to the blonde. His fingers untwist the wire holding the cork to the neck of the bottle, and pop open the bottle. As the foam flows out, he pours the bubbling champagne into the cups tilted by beautiful hands. Flushed with pride, he takes one cup from her and touches the other with it in celebration.

The waitress straightens and marches to the table. She stands in front of Ramesh, tubular arms akimbo and wide-open eyes furious. She scribbles impatiently and pulls out a piece of paper. She plants the paper on the table, in front of his face.

"Twenty guilders?" he mumbles, horrified. He pushes the note over the table.

"Corkage!" The blonde says in halting English.

"What the fuck!" He clenches his fist as he stares up at the waitress.

A thick finger points at his face. If the waitress wanted to, she could lift him by the collar and watch his arms and legs flail helplessly. Ramesh must have realised it for he backs off immediately.

He removes his fake LV wallet from inside his jacket and gabbles. The blonde translates into Dutch. The waitress bends over his hand holding pieces of paper. The money passes to the waitress, but I'm not sure I recognise it. The colours are too light, and the paper cheap and yellowish. The waitress hesitates and returns the money. Ramesh pushes them back into her hand.

He tells the blonde. "This is my country's currency. One dollar is eighty cents in guilders. I gave up forty dollars. That's more than twenty guilders." The words twist fluently.

"She wants guilders only."

"You tell her I've only dollars."

Another exchange begins between contrastable ladies. To and fro rapidly, the seductive voice and the brusque voice take turns, to make their cases, like two saws acting on cue from each other. Suddenly, the plump hand seizes the notes, and a smile lights up the dour face above. Gluttonous fingers line the notes methodically, inside an oblongish purse held by the other hand.

The couple are by themselves. Ramesh pours more champagne. They sip up the expensive fluid and lay the empty cups on their sides.

"How many days more you have?" the girl asks distantly, her sexiness accentuated by the nasal accent.

"I leave the third evening after this. I'll be back before the month is over; earlier if the clerk helps."

"Bring guilders. The money you gave me last time: hard to change into guilders."

"Don't worry. I understand." His face is full of sympathy.

"Are you happy with service last night?" Her eyelids lift wickedly. She shakes shimmering tresses before his transfixed eyes.

"Oh yes, I've never met someone like you. And don't call it service again. You are my princess."

Ramesh reaches out and holds her hand. He stares at the red nails. A cunning smile shows on his thick lips as lust dims the deep-set eyes.

The waitress gives a start and walks meekly to the old man. The wrinkled unshaven face looks up and grumbles, "Heineken!" before she can reach his table. (She has forgotten to take his order.) She turns carefully and trundles back, down the aisle which is too narrow for her.

"Heineken, Heineken," she mutters, afraid to forget again.

She speaks to the thin man at the counter. He listens attentively and disappears. He reappears with both hands holding an empty glass and a bottle of Heineken. He stands them on the round tray. The waitress lifts the plastic tray and walks to the old man, carefully keeping it level.

She puts the glass on his table and holds the green bottle unsteadily. She pours the beer slowly, the foam filling up three quarters of the glass. The old man stares and pays. He offers a tip, but she returns it, knowing service has been bad.

She turns left and right, looking for the wider aisle. She lumbers along it to the spot she always stands. She returns the tray on the counter, then places one hand over the other on her pelvis. Her eyelids get heavy and shut gradually.

A childish face presses on the windowpane. The nose and lips flatten like sitting dough as the man's face turns white. A hag's face with locks of grey hair appears at its side and turns white too. Shrivelled hands pound the glass panel, and the old idiots with squashed eyes start to laugh. The faces pull back to talk about people in the restaurant.

The timid man stops fidgeting, puts his cigarette on the ashtray and gesticulates wildly. The waitress' eyes open slowly. She gives a tired shout, and sways as quickly as she can to the door. The two faces disappear as she arrives. The timid man lifts the connecting top to chase, but lowers it back when he changes his mind. He picks up his cigarette, and the smoke drifts to the centre of the room.

***

Outside, they still sit on bollards, stand around; smoke, exchange stuff. Passersby barely notice the men and a dopey woman keeping to themselves.

The waitress recognises someone and pulls the door open. A sweet opium smell slips in as she shouts into the street. She steps aside for a shifty-looking man wearing a black hat. It's the black who took my money. His long arm receives yellowish notes from the timid man. A brief exchange later, he disappears.

A strain on the blonde's face replaces its naughtiness. I look for clues of what is happening. Ramesh's face is sweaty, eyes lecherous. His upper body shifts with care. Beneath the table: excess. A trouser leg is pulled to the knee and unclothed flesh is caressing two curvy bare thighs. The outside of his lower right leg, then the inside is sucking any moisture it can. A dark sock covers the left foot like a voyeur's mask. On the floor lie his working shoes with soles at least three inches thick.

The old man turns cautiously and looks behind him under the table. His face jerks up to cover his drink. He can't keep his mind from what is going on. Whenever I hear soft strange sounds, the face shakes automatically.

Maybe, the alcohol has numbed Ramesh's brain. Soon the waitress will see the disrespect and give him a good bashing. I would be happy to see that. If someone else is the Purser, the rest of the trip would be better.

The blonde pushes back her chair. Ramesh looks worried. She stands.

"I've to go. See you next trip."

"Don't. I can't do without you." He looks up at the taunting blue eyes.

"Can't do it here. Next trip, in the room."

"How about later?"

"I'm booked."

"You're so popular. I'll pay more if you stay."

The blonde thinks, frowning.

"Okay. But not that currency."

"I don't have any other currency."

"Sorry!" She takes her purse.

"Okay, I write you a cheque. I give you a business cheque. It won't be dishonoured."

The blonde smiles more seductively. Ramesh takes out his leather wallet and a cheque from it. He takes a pen from his jacket and writes the cheque with a flourish. The old man comments loudly. The blonde releases a torrent of Dutch, as loudly. The old face plunges back at the beer and stays silent. Ramesh pours the rest of the fizzling champagne for himself and the blonde. He gives the cheque.

"But I want guilders!"

"Helene, you can't have a guilder cheque! My company isn't in Holland."

"I'm glad to accept your cheque. But see you tomorrow. I meet a Japanese friend later."

"Okay, okay, let me kiss you before you go."

He stands and hugs her midriff for some time. She pushes his shoulders away and lowers her cheeks. As Ramesh kisses her like a last chance, the sweeping blonde tresses interlock with his black Afro-wig, creating a weird and beautiful sight. Short arms go round her tall neck, but longish hands take them apart and place them at his sides.

"*Ik hou van jou!* I love you!" She giggles.

Her sensual bare back gets onto the street.

***

A nagging hole opens. Everyone seems go back to what they always do. They sleep at night, wake up in the morning and come to the restaurant. The timid man sits at the counter. The waitress balances on wobbly legs. I walk the same route each time I'm in Amsterdam. Ramesh writes cheques. The old man wonders how long his beer would last.

I regret Ramesh won't be in trouble. Now that his woman left, he'll behave and the waitress would've no reason to slap him. His chair shifts. Once he leaves, there's no hope for a good flight home.

His stoned eyes fall on the vertical object by the counter. It doesn't know it's being watched. The propped up mass falls forward, but with a start, recovers. Chubby cheeks shake, and a hand wipes saliva off the double chin.

Ramesh smiles at me but still doesn't recognise me. He's tipsy. He raises a hand. I pray he will snap the fingers again, but the hand falls languid.

"Waitress!"

She doesn't hear.

"Coffee!" he calls louder.

"*Koffie*," the timid man squeaks, "Yvonne! …"

The waitress opens her eyes at the frightened man. He points at Ramesh. "Koffie, koffie!"

Her unkempt head nods, and he rushes into the kitchen. He is back with the coffee, yelling. He lowers his voice, self-conscious. The waitress drags a leg to the counter. Solemn faced, she lifts the glass of coffee with one hand and the long spoon with the other. She walks to Ramesh, and puts the coffee on the far side of the table and the spoon beside it. She struggles to take two sugar sachets from her side pocket and lays them by the spoon.

Ramesh pays in guilders, and the waitress returns the change in coins. He takes all the coins. His eyes follow her massive back retreat to the counter.

"You don't serve coffee in a glass," he says loudly, leaning back. He turns around to me. "It's always in a cup on a saucer: a teaspoon at one side, sugar at the other."

These are familiar words parroted by some smug colleagues. They think it's an absolute only the very privileged learn from the West. Ramesh is lucky I'm the only one here who understands English. If not, he would surely be the unhappy protagonist in a real-life comedy. I want to say: even safety issues depend on cost and comfort. What you pay is what you get!

At the end, I don't want attention. I don't want him to recognise me. His mind is clearing. He is sipping coffee which will make him alert soon.

I reach the door and push it open. It creaks.

***

"Do I know you?"

I turn. Recognition brightens his eyes. Below a long nose, thick lips become undulating pancakes. He's happy to see me, but "relieved" is a better word. His hand stretches out like a star's.

"Come, Liu," he continues like a Purser on board. I sit where the blonde had sat. He is charming. "I miss you guys. I've been very busy. She went home to see her parents. She gave me a card on board and asked if I'd call her. Why shouldn't I? Just admit she is gorgeous! Last night, she bought me dinner at our hotel and stayed overnight. I repaid her with a good shag."

English words come forth: flowery, twisting and turning, and cruising. He leaves no space for me to talk. Normally, I'm thankful for that but not now. The waitress comes. He waits while I order tea, and resumes his glibness. I pay when the tea arrives. He slows. This time I'm not losing the chance to speak.

"That blonde: I didn't see her on the flight."

"She's not in your zone."

"I would've noticed. Don't bullshit!"

"Hullo! You guys are not like me. Even the AP is different. I walk anywhere. I do what I want. You've to work. You think you see what I see?"

"Nothing escapes my eyes."

He relates how he noticed a beauty on her seat. He woke her up to talk as he didn't want to wait. She had water only and slept till landing. (She travelled from Tokyo earlier.) I look unimpressed.

"You don't trust your Purser. Frankly, I've a report on you. It's my duty …"

"Ramesh, you know something?"

"Forget what I just said. I only want a favour. I used up my guilders. I'll return you in the hotel."

I think of the things I saw him do, and the things people told me he did. He has done these so often he can't remember whom he had done it to.

"What guarantee can you give me?"

"I'll write a cheque. It's proof."

"I want something real if you don't pay up. Something convenient. Not a piece of paper. I'm not that dumb blonde."

He is very angry. I see it clearly, but he smiles. His lips quiver.

"What do you mean?"

I drink up my tea. He sips his coffee. Monkey see, monkey do! I take my time to answer. I feel the caffeine sharpening my mind.

"'F' you!" I say calmly.

"What? Insubordination! I'm writing you in."

"It's your word against mine."

He's nobody. He can only wait for the flight to have his revenge. Everyone feels the tension between us. The waitress sways past, nearby.

I don't underestimate Ramesh. How people like him work is familiar in the peninsula and island. Servile and sycophantic as underdogs or when needing help, they're often ruthless and ungrateful on top. There are clearly dire consequences for unsettling Ramesh, but problems really important are always about existence. People can be handled mostly, and I only have to make him understand it's not in his interest to muck around.

Ramesh speaks again. Then, out of frustration, he raises his glass and sniffs the coffee to show his worldliness. A sachet of sugar lies unused. He tears off a corner and empties the content into the coffee. The long spoon stirs to even out the sugar. With a tissue taken from the back of his trousers, he wipes off the stain left by the spoon on the table. He picks up the sachets and their corners, and dabs up the sugar. He folds the tissue carefully over the sachets, looking responsible. Rising, he lifts the chair quietly behind him as his thighs pushes it rearwards.

The door creaks open. The black swaggers to the counter with yellow notes in his hand. The timid man and the waitress huddle with confused faces. Ramesh hurries to leave quietly. The black scampers along the aisle and blocks the door.

***

"Let me pass," Ramesh says matter-of-factly.

The black's bloodshot eyes twitch menacingly.

"Open that door!" Ramesh points wildly, but the much taller man grins. Ramesh pulls the black's forearm. With a light wrench, the man breaks free. Ramesh steps back. He feels something and turns around. The waitress stands there: a wall of terror.

"Don't sit there. Help!" he squeaks at me.

The waitress thrusts the notes into his shirt pocket. He almost falls. The "money" sticks out stubbornly.

"*Wah*, ghost notes!"

"Call the police. These people are dangerous."

"Why should I? You'll be arrested yourself."

"I'm set up." Fear shows even on his dark face.

"Let me see your wallet."

"You know I've run out of money." He gives a show of dignity.

"Guilders," the waitress screams, holding out her hand. The black bolts the door with a thud.

"I've to ask you to be civil," Ramesh says politely. "Ma'am, guilders … no problem." He waves at me. "Liu, please lend me twenty guilders. I expect you to be on my side."

"I told you. I want something solid."

"Trust me."

"Just give her a cheque."

"No."

"Your cheques are duds."

"Shut up!"

"Thousands of afterlife dollars bought with a dollar …"

"Stupid! Don't talk like that in front of them."

"They don't understand English. Ha! Ha! We burn these notes as offering to the dead. You gave them to the living for services."

"I'm not in the mood to joke."

The waitress pulls Ramesh up by the collar with both hands. His face disappears into his jacket. The old man shouts. She releases the body. Ramesh sits on the bare floor. His Afro-wig lying like a dead rat, he is the Purser with short hair.

I get up from my chair. Approaching his body, I bend over. A pesticide-laced jungle smell chokes my nose and brain. Thick soles and a dog jaw jut out. Large black eyes are blank, and his mouth opens. The tongue shows. Suddenly, he looks like a dog panting.

"Pull me gently."

I pull him up carefully. He tucks in his crumpled shirt and pulls the trouser legs down over his shoes. He opens his fingers and combs his matted hair, touching here and there.

"Guilders," the waitress screams again and gives his chest a slight push. I pull him in time.

"Don't worry. This man will give you guilders." His raised thumb jerks at me.

"He's not my friend," I say in English slowly.

A shadow of recognition falls on the black's face. He gabbles. I worry he would act rashly. He carries a chair from a table and pushes its back against the door. He sits on it and takes out the knife. The switchblade flicks open and close as he grins from ear to ear.

"Keep that away," Ramesh says, shaking violently. The slight twists and turns in words get pronounced. "What age is this? Problems can be talked over. It's little money. I've been changing them for pounds in London. I can't force this man to help. But I fly here monthly and always stay in the same five-star Hotel. I bring the guilders once I get there."

It's difficult to comprehend twisting staccato. The others look even more confused. The old man curses. The black continues to flick his knife. The roguish face is always grinning.

"Don't be 'unbrave'," the black says, in English wryly, plunging the knife between his thighs.

The blade tip embeds in the wooden seat. The handle quivers. Ramesh catches my elbow. He waves at the street frantically, but the timid man runs to the window and pulls the curtain across. The man dashes back in the dimness, to sit by the counter nervously.

I say to the black, slowly, "If you don't put that knife away, I will tell the police you robbed me."

His fingers press the blade deftly into the handle. To my relief, the knife slips into his trouser pocket.

"I must go. This is a mistake," Ramesh says.

He takes brave looking steps towards the door. A soft shriek emerges as the waitress's massive fist swings at the side of his head. Ramesh falls sideways, after failing to catch my arm. He sits on the floor, short legs apart. The face looks dazed and, as if powdered white. Blood trickles onto his jacket, from a broken swell on his right cheek.

I bend over the red cut. He flinches, thinking I'm going to touch it. It doesn't look really bad. "Let me ask for some dressing. We have to cover it."

Without warning, his body becomes soft, and his head sways. "Get an ambulance."

The waitress's eyes soften too. I point at Ramesh's bloody cheek, and pat the space above it. He smarts again. The old man hobbles over. He peers at the pitiful figure like it's dying. The timid man arrives with a first aid box.

"Must I repeat I need an ambulance?" Ramesh screams. From the sitting position, his body falls slowly onto the floor. His head slumps to a rest. The face turns on one side and saliva flows.

I've the feeling something's not right. The eyeballs twitch beneath flesh shutters, and his limbs move minutely. His body has also settled with care.

The worried faces look down at the body. It's mumbling, "Ambulance, ambulance."

Those words give hope.

"'Armbullan'?" the black asks suddenly, still on his chair. "What is armbullan?"

"Doctor! He wants a doctor."

The black stands and pulls back the curtain. He snatches the first aid box from the timid man. The old man feels Ramesh's chest. He shouts he feels heartbeats. He shouts Ramesh is breathing. The waitress's face relaxes. The black opens the box, and the timid man points out each item to explain its function. The waitress lowers her hippo body, beside Ramesh's puny chest. Her massive hand covers his forehead and caresses it. She grunts he has no fever and looks at all eyes to be sure everyone understands.

***

I find myself back at the hotel before I left it. Against my will, I try to connect the status quo to what happened. *I was in the room, all alone. What was I doing?* I had left the room when I couldn't handle the thing. I normally do this in the situation. To stay and tackle the thing squarely likely brings nothing but more pain. I needed space to handle the thing but, as expected, events overtook me. I can still return of course … . *It was the dream. I must know what was in the dream.*

The waitress has stood up. The old man too. The timid man is holding the box again. Have they seen through Ramesh's hoax he is dying?

I have an idea. It's my dream again. *Something!* I think about what the dream was but the idea disappears. Some interruption to my concentration I can't finger (as I'm not focused), caused this loss.

I look at Ramesh. He's frowning. He gives a soft cry and clutches his chest. They surround him quickly; the black kneeling, after snatching the box and laying it on the floor. The black takes a thermometer and stretches Ramesh's cheeks with the fingers of his other hand. The hand pushes open Ramesh's lower jaw. The glass stick digs Ramesh's mouth and nestles under the tongue. The waitress knees by his body. She places the heel of a palm on his sternum, just above the notch. The other heel sits on top of the hand.

She rises on her knees and bends forwards. I want to stop her, but more ideas about the dream appear. Next moment, the massive chest jerks downwards. The huge arms and hands moved first, like a powerful pump.

Ramesh jerks and yells as I hear a crackling sound. He sits up and holds his chest. Then he falls backwards, writhing in pain.

I kneel before his body immediately. I unbutton and open his shirt. An ominous line lies across a darker area on his chest. Thick bright blood oozes over a half-centimetre shard at the end of a line.

"Call an armbullan," I shout.

"Armbullan. What armbullan?"

"Doctor, call a doctor!"

The timid man runs to the counter and lifts the handle on the black phone. He turns the dial, cursing each time it takes its time to return, before he dials again. Then he shrieks excitedly, below his hand, into the mouthpiece.

Ramesh's cries become a whimper. He falls silent. He is unconscious. It's real this time. When I lift his eyelid, the pupil looks dead. I run to the phone, grab a thick directory and put it under his head. The thick blood continues to flow: not fast but steady enough to cause alarm. The viscosity over the bone pulsates. His chest heaves weakly, a sign he is breathing. We only have to wait.

At once, regret sweeps over me. I would've prevented this stage of Ramesh's tragedy, if I had heeded my instinct and responded straightaway. Yet I realise this is again, not a time to think. With an immense effort (eased by the sense of urgency), I sweep the thought away. I'm relieved it works. I daren't think about it. It's too risky to think now.

I hear the siren wailing like a cat on heat, in the bright afternoon. My heart races as blue lights whirl. The black unbolts the door and opens it. The ambulance crew pronounces Ramesh's condition is critical. He must be in hospital. I write "Hotel Okura" on a piece of paper and give it to the driver. They will find out the airline he's working for and look for its manager.

All of us have become friends, united by the mission to save Ramesh. We look on sadly as the ambulance bumps away along the undulating alleys of Dam Square. The waitress is even crying. I don't mention the robbery to anyone, and no one mentions Ramesh's twenty guilder scam.

I want to go back to the hotel, but I'm loathe to face the thing. I trudge along the cobbled streets of Dam square, self-absorbed again.

***

Ramesh won't die, but it is likely he won't be able to fly anymore. Flying home without him gets real, but would be unpleasant if I'm wrecked by guilt. I keep thinking I should've obeyed the instinct to let those thoughts go. If I couldn't let go, I should've the guts to do so. And if I still couldn't, I should've the will to be able to force myself. Still, I feel I shouldn't be blamed for lacking conviction the situation was serious enough to throw those thoughts. It's excusable to feel there could be something to get from the thoughts. But I didn't get anything! Was there nothing, and I had wasted precious time finding? I can't say I failed by chance due to a concentration lapse. Alas, I've achieved nothing again, and it was my fault again.

I'm putting my woes aside and rise above the situation. Anything below it wouldn't matter once the new situation turns out fine. I think, perhaps, Ramesh will appreciate I've gone through this ordeal with him. He may realise all of us tried to save him, and each played our part. He may realise, at last, life is more than self-centredness. But he may think I was stingy over twenty guilders, and that caused his ruin. If he were allowed to continue to fly, I suppose he would want revenge. Or, his friends might blame me if he has to leave. They would come after me. Unfortunately, I don't possess anything I can hold against him.

I've missed the chance at preventing a human disaster, but Ramesh really deserves more. I hold no grudges against him now. He has paid for his sins even if it was incomplete. Or did he merely satisfy my selfish cry for revenge? Or my soft-hearted weakness? I feel sorry for him. I can't forget the things he did, but I can always forgive him. I will do him the favour of keeping his shame from the public and crews. Unless, if and when he returns to flying, he continues to be a bastard to the crews. …

In fact, it's why I wrote.

Chapter 10
Anything Can Happen

I wake up and reach the window of my flat, on the twelfth floor, to open it a little as my mind begins its automatic task of tidying and rearranging. It churns in a ghostly washing machine: squinting, smirking and shifting – like art! Strong winds sweep in through the gap, stinging my dazed face with cold painful water. I slam the glass window shut and yank down the latch. The dim lighting from congested flats opposite and street lights below, show the longish hands on the partially lit clock, hanging at the top of the wall, at five in the morning.

I had arrived on a flight in the late afternoon. The heavy downpour started at nightfall. Amorphous thoughts shifted in my mind, as I tried to reposition them during the night. When they were lifted, stacked and properly arranged, I washed up and went to sleep.

Now amidst the heavy rain with constant thunder and incessant lightning, the mind is moving again. Soon, I will be on the hot seat as usual: consciously looking for preferred decisions, careful not to make wrong ones. This gloomy weather is making me imagine the worst scenarios, but I can't even think about them. As the thoughts gather pace with increasing intensity, I feel worse and worse because I don't have a chance to imagine them.

I hear footsteps mounting the staircase outside, before the hissing sound of a thick newspaper being shoved through under the door. My eyes adjust to the face of a glamorous-looking Chinese girl on the front page of the paper I'm holding against the kitchen light. I catch sight of the headline: *Air Hostess's Body Washed Ashore.* I realise the familiar face belongs to Howard's lover, and my eyes attack the words below: *The dead body of a young woman was found lying yesterday morning, on the shore of Marina Esplanade. She was only in tattered panties. There were no signs of foul play, but police have arrested an airline Purser on suspicion of involvement in murder. Investigations are ongoing. Anyone with information can call ...*

I get the message of course. But did I miss something? My mind whirling, I had returned to the lines, left and returned again, leaving dark spots. I read them again, to cover those spots. At the word "yesterday", my attention takes leave as my eyes glance at the surrounding words. My attention returns at "tattered", goes somewhere and returns again. Unhappy with what I did, I read the passage again. At "yesterday", it takes off again and somewhere else, the same happens again. I read the sentences again, and it happens again. There's something, I feel, I still miss. If only I had concentrated! Maybe I miss more than the something. With desperate effort, I gather the thoughts and fling them over my shoulder, and find myself asking if I have indeed lost nothing. I throw that last thought over the shoulder as well and tell myself if I've lost something, so be it. Then I throw that over too and ask myself something else. ...

I see the thoughts on the floor. The picture of Howard at the back of my mind gets nasty. Claws are growing and reaching out from it. I think, surely, there's something to do even though his lover is dead. How about Connie? I should try to see if she needs help, but I can't think clearly what to do. In fact, I can't see why she should be helped. I'm afraid I hadn't read those lines properly. This would affect my understanding of the situation and Connie's well-being. I could have missed insights, especially ontological ones. If I don't read the lines again, I would miss out entirely since incomplete information is useless. Missing wouldn't be one but both types of stuff. Then the debate rages whether I should accept and move on. The more I try to close the gap, the more I'm left behind. I think I should, now, be handling those thoughts in my mind before the paper came early on. But I've to do something for Connie. Yet Connie is safe. I should deal with matters one at a time. Why didn't I do that? I've wasted enough time already. I should do something, not waste more time. The more I think, the more time I waste, but nothing is ever a waste of time.

Anything can happen, I feel. Maybe the clock will fall with a loud clang, and break into pieces. The second hand takes the role of the minute hand. At each tick, a minute passes. The minute hand is the hour hand. Time is rushing, but I can't move. It cannot slow down for me. It leaves me further and further behind.

I sit on the sunken orange sofa in the living room, my buttocks hurt by wooden slats beneath. In front of me, after the low table, a wall of red bricks stands on textured wallpaper. On my right, the dim world outside the window glass is overlaid with reflections of a television and the bricks. Everything in the room appears to exist inside wallpaper, at this time, this morning. A worker can easily tear down the wall, if he were told to do so, and put up another picture.

I walk to the wall, adjoining the door behind and flip down a switch. The windowpane lights up as an orange brightens the room. I hold the newspaper up to the translucent ball with a bright bulb inside. An amorphous disc lights up the dead girl's face. I don't feel the emotion I should have, and grip the paper tightly for it to surface. The sensation is odd.

Soft sounds come from the long kitchen situated after the tall altar table. My father is making hot Ovaltine for himself before going for work. I hear the spoon, held by his strong hand, stir the beverage in the cup gently. He has walked past me from the other room, and switched on the white light in the kitchen, but I've not noticed. He asks me, in the Fuqing dialect, if I want breakfast.

He seems, oddly, to be talking out of another piece of wallpaper. I'm used to not answering him, though I've promised myself, many times, to speak to him. I know I have not been reasonable. I've been rebellious, familiar and troubled. Unanswered issues are blocking me, besides not being able to speak our dialect.

I hear barefoot steps behind me, crossing the reddish brown room on the poorly laid ceramic tiles. Now, he is bending and putting on his shoes at the door. *Pa, wait! Don't work too hard!* But words don't come as I face the bricks. He steps out of the paper box. I hear the door close. My heart sinks. He has forgotten to switch off the kitchen light. I'll do it for him. No, I didn't forget: I am still thinking.

Howard is suspected of murder, but he may not have done it. I remember my mind flitted away before it returned as I said those words. The paper would be saying the following if I had a normal degree of focus: *maybe he didn't do it, but it's possible he did.* In fact, both sentences have the same content, but only one is more accurate. One also says more than the other. *I think he didn't do it. The girl probably killed herself. But why did the police suspect Howard?* I find to my dismay, I have again said it differently. This has wider meaning and more opinions. What did I just say? I think I said: *But why did the police suspect Howard? I think he didn't do it. The girl probably killed herself.* All the sentences contain the same words in the same order, but the former's changed positions make different emphases. So which is accurate understanding? Which is correct understanding? How words are said affects understanding! What words are thought to mean, affects understanding! But without words, I cannot think. I can't think of any instance in which my insight has nothing to do with words. This is still the case when I try to understand the intuitive experience. All the distorted understandings add up to what? Many problems again. I can't face them at the same time, but I couldn't easily focus on one either. By default, I focus on one.

Against my wishes, I slip my wallet into the back of my shorts. I continue to defy myself as my feet walk to the door and slip into the flip-flops. I push open the door, step out of the flat and close it. I push the knob to be sure the door is locked. Pulling my comb from the back pocket, I tidy my hair quickly with it. I climb the steps, reach the landing and turn round to mount another flight. Then I turn right along the lighted corridor to the grey lift and press the button.

I hear slippers being dragged towards me. From the corner of my eye, I see the man who lives on the other side of the lift. I do not look at him as I don't want to disrupt my train of thoughts.

"Have you eaten?" he asks in Fujian dialect as I look at the floor. He doesn't get the message to mind his business. "How's flying? You're so lucky. You've been to all parts of the world. Which country do you like best?"

Everyone takes the opportunity to ask me the same questions when we meet. Before I was seen in uniform, no one bothered to look at me even when I passed. It's different now! At first, I had felt flattered. Then I became irritated. Now fangs take shape in my head. I want to snarl at the stubborn, busybody face. But I don't do it. Perhaps I can't. Why? Perhaps it can't be done. I have to accept it can't be done because I just can't do it. I'm one of the few people who can't do it.

The lift arrives loudly and opens like it's coughing. I step inside the claustrophobic box and wait for the man to enter. I press the button. I step over a blot of drying phlegm and slink into the corner. Notwithstanding the stench of stale urine, I stare at the closed door in front.

The graffiti-laden doors jerk and open. I step out into the dull light, self-absorbed. Beyond the void deck, the floor is covered with a crinkled sheet of water. The rising sun gives the rain a whiteness as it flashes off the cement floor like desperate fishes. I realise I have forgotten it's raining and didn't bring an umbrella. I stand away from the edge of the rain under shelter of the ceiling as a tinge of regret gathers. The seductive pain offers sweet comfort.

The combined forces of the other problems pushes back. *Similar poles repel*, I whisper in relief. Long ago, this happened. Whenever an abstract problem remained unsolved and another appeared, either the former or the latter lost its hold, since there was space in my mind for only one problem. But I began to ask if it might not always be the case. I started having flashes of this possibility whenever two problems coexisted. Eventually on occasions, the repulsion of like poles didn't work. Then it happened more and more often. Finally, when a problem appeared in the presence of others, they all became interconnected, and the new problem was added. This is a rare occasion, when either a new problem or an old one gets neutralised.

The regular beats and gunpowdery smell of the rain exude a soporific quality. I wonder whether it's all right to continue in a state where thoughts don't matter. White lines still strike the floor hard and make loud pelting sounds. The rain is so empty, yet mystical as I stand motionless like a statue. Thoughts stand still and recede into the background as they get left behind.

Suddenly, the rain slows as a growl of thunder rolls over the building. The vertical lines thin and gentle, the jumps are tamed.

A slightly rotund man walks onto the dry void deck. Rainwater slides off the top of the open umbrella tilted over his head. He pulls in the fragile shelter to close it, then shakes it at the floor to dislodge the water. This neat-looking man with mild eyes, lives opposite my flat on the same corridor. He is younger than my father, and they speak in the Fuzhou dialect when they meet. He looks up at me and smiles, a gold-lined incisor gleaming from a set of good teeth.

"I met your father this morning. He was going to work." He speaks gently in Mandarin. "So you came back from overseas?"

"I woke up early." I'm always polite to him.

"Where did you fly from? *Wah*, so lucky. You have been to every part of the world."

"I came down for breakfast, but it's raining."

"Have you been to Taiwan? Why didn't you bring your umbrella?" He looks at me like he pities me for being limited by youthful insouciance.

"Yes, I've been there many times. Nice place. The rain has stopped. I'm going. Too hungry."

"Take my umbrella."

"No, too troublesome. Thanks a lot."

I wave at him as I walk into the cold drizzle. He shakes his head and winces.

***

My hand shelters my damp head, as I wait for a car to reverse into a parking lot. I cross the road, tread on the sheltered walkway and stand on the wet "five-foot way". My bare hand wipes water from my face before I enter the large coffee shop.

The regular faces are already there, fresh despite the early rain. Some of the people will travel to work when they leave, while others walk to the nearby market. The largest stall at the centre selling drinks, and two other stalls open early. I stand with other customers in front of the fishball noodles stall, at this end of the hall and wait for my chance to speak to the vendor.

The warm odorous air from the stall makes me flinch in the chilly humidity. The honest-looking man in a white T-shirt – tiny beads growing on his neck and face – works rapidly. A ladle scoops soup one moment, fishballs another; hands gather sorts of noodles one moment, other ingredients another, and after that, doing other little chores. The humming fan standing beside him, provides scant relief. He doesn't pause as he hovers like a bee, eyeing the tools of his trade, and he takes orders and banters.

A woman grumbles in Fujian. "Tell the *ah soh* auntie bringing the food, I am at the end there. No fishball, no fish cake, no fish soup, no lard: lean pork only."

"You want noodles or not?"

"Yes! *Mee pok* flat noodles, dry."

"I sell fish foods," the man jokes in Fujian and some Teochew. "Lucky, she wants noodles. Otherwise, what do I sell?"

She scowls and pouts her lips.

"Soup *mee* noodles for me," I say with a stern face and hope he appreciates my simplicity. "I'm sitting by your stall, right here."

I sit next to a middle-aged couple at the bare table. At the next round table, the middle-aged "coffee boy" has dispensed drinks from his tray and is listening intently to fresh orders.

"I want tea, less milk," a man says.

"Coffee with evaporated milk, lots of sugar," his wife interjects in Cantonese. "And two slices of bread with *kaya* and margarine, toasted. Not too black. Two eggs, half-boiled."

The coffee boy nods and shuffles to the other table. His black hair is tousled and his bony face is lean like his body. His white singlet and blue shorts are rather stained.

"Drinks?" he asked, expecting many orders.

"'Kick ball, kill germs'. Dark bread, steamed. Ten slices altogether. Cut into triangles."

"I want a packet of tissues. How much is it?"

"Fifteen cents," the answer shoots out.

"Wah! Ten cents, can?"

"Standard price, *hor!*"

"Two for twenty-five cents, can? Elder brother, you want one to bring to office?"

"No, I prefer old-fashioned handkerchief."

"Sorry, ask *towkay* boss. He is leaving soon. I am only a *kopi* boy." Irritation flickers.

"No need. One packet enough."

The coffee boy twists to stand in front of my table. He blinks as he focuses on remembering what were ordered and what would be ordered.

"Tea, thick," I say, looking at his confident face with admiration. He doesn't need a writing pad like crew members on board.

"Two coffees black, *kopi-o*: one thick, one thin. Lots of sugar for the first one. No sugar for the second one," the lady next to me says.

The coffee boy walks on, scanning the tables for used articles which he removes.

This man started work two hours ago and will be here for eight more hours. He'll have a quick meal which he doesn't pay and sits at one of the tables when he is free. He does this every day except Sundays, and his monthly pay is only one hundred and fifty dollars. When his parents died, he had left primary school. He now supports two younger brothers and a sister. At forty, he is still a bachelor.

No girls like to marry a disadvantaged man who knows little English, foisted on the population by a few (with lies and half-truths) to win power. The noodles vendor is also disadvantaged by English, as he employs others.

The coffee boy balances the heavy items on the tray, expertly. He serves the items, smoothly, from one table to another.

The man at my table raises a hand. He scolds the coffee boy for overcharging. The server explains, without unease, how the sum was arrived. The man realises his mistake and gives the coffee boy a ten dollar note. He wants to make compensation with part of the change. The coffee boy gives coins, from his tray, to the man. He says he will be back with the rest of the change, and won't make money out of a small misunderstanding. He strides to the drink stall as his eyes sweep the tables clean again. He returns with small notes, for the contrite man.

The rain has stopped. Some Chinese customers stand in front of the Tamil stall, at the other end of the coffee shop. A Malay family ambles to the empty table on my right and pulls out five wooden chairs. One of the two boys drags three chairs from other tables. The parents are in their late thirties. The man, in a grungy airline overall, looks tired. The others, round in bright clothes, appear to have just got out of bed and are going for a picnic. They put their light bags on two chairs, and wait for the man to speak.

A white Eurasian in a tight-fitting T-shirt and blue jeans strolls in, a newspaper folded under a heavily tattooed arm. His long black hair is tied into a pony tail at the back of his head. He sits at the table the Malay boy took the chairs from. The young, well-tanned Asian girl in a low-cut dress, next to him, has been waiting for him. The middle-aged man doesn't work. He walks about the neighbourhood in slippers any time in a day. His family has emigrated to Australia. He lives alone in one of the blocks nearby. He is often with a woman for a few months before he is seen with another.

He waves at the Indian stall-holder and shouts. "*Thamby!* Two *pratas* for each of us. All *kosong*, no egg. One mutton curry."

At once, the oily man's head shakes like on a spring. Expert hands press and knead the dough on the slippery top. He speaks Tamil to his fat helper. The Malay family still can't decide what to order. The girl with a big bosom, who is oldest and about eighteen, looks at the Eurasian and giggles. He notices and smiles back. Her father chastises her in Malay.

The Eurasian beckons the coffee boy by waving his hand downwards. "*Kopi-o* for two, Malboro: one. And the kopi-o: more sugar for one; just a little less sugar than the first one for the other one."

"What you say?" the coffee boy shouts back.

"Remember yesterday? Same as yesterday's."

The helper, his potbelly in front, comes with two plates of pratas and a dish of mutton curry, before those waiting longer are served. He gives the Eurasian separate curry, two pairs of forks and spoons, and two serviettes. Gold gleams in his nimble mouth as he twists and turns English words slipping out. He rubs his crotch and looks at the slim girl paying. He smiles lecherously after his big eyes observe the Eurasian is looking elsewhere.

The Malay waves at him and orders for the family. The man tells his bosomy daughter to buy drinks and gives her money. She stands abruptly and walks slowly to the counter. She returns with four cans of Coke in her hands. Behind her, the Chinese lady from the drinks stall, balances six glasses filled with ice-cubes on a tray.

***

The Eurasian spreads the paper into a broadsheet. He reads aloud: "Air hostess's body washed …"

All the thoughts I had upstairs crowd into my mind. The world in front of me and the coffee shop steps back and shrinks and blurs. …

What are the issues? The important ones! It has to do with the news about Howard. It has to do with how words distort meaning and understanding. Yet more important, waiting for an answer, is something else. Something totally to do with Howard and Connie. And before that, last night of course. There is difficulty retrieving that piece of information, though I know what it is. I should get it if I try hard enough, but it's difficult when I can't concentrate on it. Most of all, I'm afraid to return to the past, to what is at the back of my mind. Afraid for various reasons … *afraid to think*. …

The world hovers from coagulation to solidity, moving to and fro, front to back as the coffee boy brings the coffees for the Eurasian and the girl. She pays again. The coffee boy looks at them and walks away. The Eurasian tastes the coffee.

I think: *Am I going to be free?* …

"*Aagh*, so concentrated!" He grimaces.

"Mine is OK. Michael, you should've told the *kopi* boy you wanted skinny coffee," she says.

"He should know. Yesterday, I had dilute coffee here. By the way; that steward, do you know him?"

"Which one?"

"The one in the paper! He killed the girl!"

"Of course! Worked with him. He's a man girls can't resist. Has lots of girlfriends: like you. Connie bailed him out last night and paid his debts."

"Did he kill that girl?"

"I don't think so. He's a nice guy. I heard they were in a hotel room before her body was found."

"Excuse me!" The Malay man has turned. He stared at the paper with reddish eyes. "The man, I know. I'm from the same airline. I met him many times on the aeroplane before take-off. This morning, the police brought him. In handcuffs like this! They asked the crew many questions. I heard they release him after that." He has the typical, gentle Malay accent.

"Why?"

"Not enough evidence, lah."

"That's good news," the girl says happily.

... *Slowly* ...

"But case's still open lah," the Malay continues. "That means if they see new evidence, they will find him again."

The Indian helper comes to the family's table with a stack of floury smelling *roti pratas*. He plonks six oily plates and a bowl of curry down on the centre, and cutlery with fingerprints next to them. The children's hands bypass the cutlery to tear the rotis. The Malay man watches tiredly and brightens. He puts two fingers on his chocolate lips and sucks air. He points at the pack in front of the girl, and reaches for the matchbox on the improvised tin-can ashtray. He takes a cigarette and lights it, as his wife grumbles and moves away.

"Maybe it's suicide," the Eurasian says.

"Was she killed by gangsters? She had powerful *Ah Beng* friends."

"Maybe the gangsters tried to kill the Purser, but the girl stopped them," the Malay says.

"Maybe, that was how she got killed."

"She was very beautiful. Even on the beach, though her body was grey and swollen with water.

She still had the airline make-up on her face. Somehow, her face managed to stay above water."

The Malay man finishes his cigarette and stretches across the Eurasian's table again. The Eurasian turns from the newspaper and sees creeping fingers. He smacks the hand, straightaway.

"Ouch! Just one more stick, *tolong*. Please!"

"*Jaga!* Watch out! No!"

The world is getting fluid again … and clear … *mustn't think …*

The family get up and carry their bags over the shoulders. The Malay sends the other girl to pay. He drags his feet towards the car park, when his wife and the three children hurry away.

I look around. The coffee boy has switched off the lights. The restaurant is quiet and dim. I'm alone at my table. Most of the customers have left, but there are one or two new faces. My table has been cleared and wiped clean. An unpleasant food smell sticks to the top.

***

"Hullo!" The Asian girl waves at the coffee boy standing, lost in thought, by the drink counter.

"What you want?"

"One more coffee. Make sure it's light this time." She assumed a British accent.

She takes a tissue from her handbag and dries the wet surface in front of Michael. She pulls another piece, dabs his mouth and admires the light face. His lips are thick and his nose is gentle like most Asians, but his eyes are deep set like Caucasians.

Glassy irises show his soul, yet she couldn't understand why he is highly prized. He has black hair like her – she is grateful – and stops the thought process to focus on the present. She notices he is more than twice her size as the *kopi* boy comes with the coffee, and Michael continues to read the paper. She pays, and the coffee boy walks away.

"Coffee too sweet!" the Eurasian scowls.

The sweet faced girl sips his coffee. "That's not too sweet, dear. You forgot to say less less sugar again."

The Eurasian's eyes search for the coffee boy, and stop where he is talking to the cleaner.

"Change this," Michael says loudly.

The server walks up to Michael. "What want?" He speaks English with disadvantaged characteristics.

"Change this to less less sugar."

"No change!"

"Call the *towkay* here!" Michael points authoritatively.

"What?"

"You cannot understand English or what?"

I tell the coffee boy in Mandarin what the man wants. I tell the English speaker the lowly server represents the boss too.

The Eurasian stands and looks at the coffee boy superciliously. He is much bigger and taller. A push would send the other man sprawling. But the man looks at Michael confidently. He is fitter and he knows that's important. They wait for each other to start. The big body jerks but pulls back. A fist rises and lowers. Michael's eyes look like firecrackers going to explode, yet he daren't make the move he wants badly. He looks at me for support.

"I never met such a guy. Everyone is so nice to me here, but this gangster is rude and unreasonable. I can break his arms anytime I want."

"I see."

"What kind of service is this? Served a wrong drink, didn't even say sorry. He just has to change the coffee, and everything would be OK."

I can't contain my irritation anymore.

"If you can't speak something he can understand, you should at least keep quiet."

The black eyebrows arch as he decides. The chest heaves, and he swallows saliva.

"He has to understand me. I'm the customer."

"Michael, don't be so arrogant," the girl says. "Give and take."

He gives her a fierce look. She looks back lovingly. *Hard love?*

A different thought slips in. I adjust … *not too much … stop thinking.* … There are opposite movements.

"That's right," I blurt out. "You're lucky to be here. Someone like you should be serving him."

The muscles under Michael's thick flesh twitch. Controlling himself, he says, "You mean he's better than me?"

"He speaks more languages than you. He can communicate with all races here, except people like you. He remembers those orders, some as silly as yours. What can you do besides using women?"

"I know who you are," his girlfriend interrupts. "Your name is Liu, right? You want me to tell the office how you behaved in public? I'll tell all the senior crew. I'll tell Richard, my Ward Leader."

A bimbo, I think.

"Want to fight?" Michael says, still standing. He lifts big round fists. He glances at me before glaring at the *kopi* boy. "Tell him to fight if he has balls."

The coffee boy stands, in front of the giant, with smaller fists. "Come *lah*. Punch lah."

Michael lumbers around, fists in front to give a fatal punch. His enemy retreats, hands open like two knives of a praying mantis. The girl thrusts herself between the men, and faces the pale Eurasian.

"Stop it. Remember your condition."

It takes a while for her message to sink in. He looks angry she embarrassed him. He is undecided. His hands fall, and he announces proudly. "I don't fight with smelly *chow Ah Bengs*."

"No 'balls' *chap cheng!*" The coffee boy smirks.

"It's not that he has no balls," I say loudly in Fujian for everyone to hear. "He dropped his *lum pahs* somewhere."

The coffee boy's finger traces an imaginary line on the floor. Michael's eyes narrowed, aiming poison sideways at me. He understands roughly what I said. Then he takes his newspaper and walks to the table by the Indian stall, at the other end. The girl follows, the pack of Malboro in her hand. She sits and snuggles to her giant toy.

The coffee shop is still quiet. Other customers have left, but a man outside is thinking whether to enter. I still see and hear the couple clearly. The morning sun casts an orange wedge on one side of the round top. Greyish shadows lengthens from the legs under the table.

"I told you many times to relax. I can't be around always to remind you. Please control yourself! Remember that heart attack after you quarrelled with the nurse. Luckily, the doctors revived you. You were hospitalised. I paid the bills. You didn't want C class. It was below your dignity, you said. You insisted on A, but I only had money for B."

"Thanks for reminding me all this. I would've taught the gangster a lesson if not for you."

"But he's used to hardship. You take *Tongkat Ali* for erection. You're no match for him, dear."

"And you've a stupid mouth. You embarrass me in public."

"It's for your own good. Grow up! You're spoilt and capricious. I love you very much! But you're crossing marriageable age?" She pats his big back like a mother. "I'm not Connie. Her family is rich, and she can spend on her boyfriend. No problem since he appreciates. She knows she will get back her money."

"You mean I don't appreciate?" He lights a cigarette to chase away the persistent fly.

"I'm mentally prepared now. So, you may leave anytime. I work hard, yet I've not been saving. I'm on five-year contracts. They say I'm like a prostitute because my value falls as I get older. Men don't like to see an old hostess, even when she smiles. The Airline knows that." Michael looks at her painfully. "Anyway, Howard was marrying Connie once he broke up with his lover …"

The Indian helper smiles. "How's the pratas? You want more?" His round face shakes as he fondles the tumescence on his sarong. "You fly ah? Flying women very beautiful."

"How do you know?"

"I listen. I open my eyes. You been many countries all over the world. Where you like best?"

"London. I love to shop at Oxford Street."

"You been India? I've house in Madras. The job is very good, you very lucky but also very hard work. I know. When you fly at night, no sleep."

"Overnight flights are very tiring."

"You've day flights to Madras? How many in one week?"

Michael sweeps the back of his hand towards the dreamy face. He turns to the girl having difficulty holding his large hand. "Don't they always ask stupid questions?"

The self-conscious helper lowers his eyelids. "You have pratas on aeroplane?"

"*Thambi*," the Eurasian says impatiently. "Enough pratas! Your curry tasted overnight?"

"You don't want more food. I go."

***

It's bright outside. Confusion and doubts have sunk. The world is as real as it can be. Three customers are left. I sit alone at the table by the noodles stall with an unhindered view of the other side. The girl nestles her head on Michael's big chest.

"You said a purser was picking on you."

She contemplates her tanned bosom below. "You mean Ali *Botak*. Luckily, I didn't fly with him after that. Everyone is terrified of the fanatic. He follows the training manual like his holy book. Anyway, something happened to him."

"You said …"

"One night, he left his jacket on the back of a seat and took his time in the First Class toilet. When he came out, the khaki jacket has a hole. He asked the crew who did it, but no one said anything. Then he questioned passengers as though they were crew members." She draws a big circle in the air with both hands. "This big!"

"You said he never picked on his kind. Does he give good reports for lousy work?"

"They help each other. But he doesn't 'try' girls like other religious bigots. Hostesses don't get away when they make mistakes. He cares for his image. He is never seen with hostesses or those of another faith. He eats before a flight lands and saves nearly every cent. His second wife is twenty years younger than himself. I heard a rumour. A Control boy was caught calling Ali and friends, during standby, for high allowance flights. This clerk wore a gold Rolex. He was transferred to another department. Ali was given a warning letter."

"*Woah*, they only transferred him."

"Some of us were sacked just for taking a pack of cards. It's about politics and connections."

"I can see flying is good money. No wonder your friend paid off Howard's debts. He is lucky. Devoted girls are relics. They really love." Michael winks to show he was joking.

"Howard's debts are huge. She wouldn't pay up if her parents didn't help."

"She used up her money on Howard first, right?"

"Who said?"

"If she didn't put in a good word for Howard, do you think the parents would help?"

Her voice rises and loses that stilted accent. It makes her more natural. "The parents met Howard and like him. Howard promised to return every cent. Even her parents saw his sincerity. Everyone knows he keeps promises."

"You are so different from Connie. You don't trust me." Michael's heavy palm falls on the table. The tin can jumps. It jolts and refreshes my mind.

He lights a cigarette and smokes it. He waves politely for a beer. He speaks humbly, this time. The can arrives quickly, together with a glass of ice cubes. He pulls off the tab and the *kopi* boy waits for payment. With a confused look, the girl finally opens her purse. She looks at Michael eventually with adoring eyes.

I raise my hand and order another "thick tea". (Sweetened condensed milk is always added.) I drink slowly – reluctant to finish it – sending waves of caffeine into my brain. My mind becomes clearer still. My heart pounds. I tell myself, *I'm doing well. ... leave it alone ...*

I look up. They are embracing each other, the Eurasian giving the girl a wide smile for the first time. "You're very beautiful."

Her voice turns soppy. "And you're handsome, so *Ang Moh* and European. Do you know? Connie said Howard and the other woman met many times to discuss breaking up. When the woman learnt Howard was a fake, she almost became insane. She couldn't accept the reality, and she couldn't leave him. She had spent too much time on Howard. Her friends knew him well and thought a perfect couple was getting married. Most of all, she was madly in love. For some time, she was furious."

I hear them clearly.

"After being cheated, she still loved him!"

"That's stupid! In fact, Howard also told Connie to leave him? But when Connie found out he was breaking up with the other girl too, she convinced him to return. Then one day, his lover shocked him by saying she accepted his past, and he had to continue to pretend. Howard refused to do so. He was determined to turn over a new leaf and go with Connie. But the other girl was stubborn. Perhaps, he told her at Hyatt his decision was final, and she killed herself."

"Howard borrows money to continue a lifestyle? Nothing's wrong with that. That's why there are credit cards."

"Flight attendants fly to famous cities and stay in classy hotels. They've access to expensive goods and services, and they're paid well. It wasn't difficult to pretend to be some big shot. Howard and that girl only had to be more organised."

There is a pause.

"I would like to come on your flight as before. You only pay for my air tickets. We save a lot on hotel bills this way."

The girl stammers, "You buy your own tickets, then you can come with me."

"OK. I pay you once you buy them."

"Why don't you go buy them yourself? I'll give you the dates and flight numbers, so you can book the flights."

"You do it. You know the people and the system. It's faster and cheaper this way."

"You haven't paid me all those money."

"Trust me. It's up to you to make it work."

The girl groans. "I gave you everything I have, literally. I do anything. But don't you love me, after all this? Do you think for me? Do you think of me?"

Her mouth opens like she's choking. The eyes are red and wet. She is suffering because of her racism. She always assumes minorities can only be victims.

"I give you attention. That's sacrifice! There are many 'sarong party girls', and you know that."

"I neglected my family who really needs me."

Her head drops against the unresponsive body, and she sobs uncontrollably. She dries her tears with a tissue herself, but the Eurasian pushes back his chair and stands. The girl stands too, and the two faces lock eyes from dissimilar heights for some time. Her beseeching face is a kaleidoscope of emotions as she pulls his shirt down. "Please sit!" She waves at the coffee boy, frantically. When he didn't see, she calls in accented Fujian like a British person. The coffee boy is by her side instantly, out of sympathy. She forces out a smile and orders another coffee.

She asks Michael, "You want another Tiger?"

My mind feels strained. Confusion and doubts eat my consciousness, casting a translucent shroud over everything in front.

He nods. They lower themselves onto the chairs, facing each other for a second time at one side of the table: the girl smiling, the big man still angry. The late morning sun casts an orange glow on the two flushed faces while under the tables, short black shadows overlay the greyish light in the hall. Amidst the sharp whispers and the cool caused by the early rain, the incongruity of the moment turns the world into wall pictures again.

Poor soul in a sweet frame carrying that pain. But she's lucky for the opportunity to go through extremes. As for myself, I've nothing to talk about, since all my experiences – as far as I can remember – are half-baked at best. Now I know I can never fully experience anything. Trouble is, hope for a change in fate never dies. Besides these personal tragedies only I see, I've nothing, but wrenching solitudes and very disturbing thoughts to free.

Wobbling, I stand and leave.

Chapter 11
A Cacophony of Noise, Smells and Activities

This scenario is typical on these flights. As people stuff baggage of all shapes and sizes into every nook and cranny during boarding, the stuffy cabin fill with overwhelming smells. The loquacious passengers harangue the crew for water to drink and other favours, and to have their seats changed.

With much acrimony, we secure the cabin and galleys for take-off. The passengers and crew are strapped, and the aircraft begins its steep and violent climb. Chimes sound non-stop from everywhere, as call lights appear all over the ceiling. The cabin looks like a fairyland from my take-off seat, but those people are saying they won't wait. The fasten seat belt signs are switched off, and we get up to sally forth and serve. The men and women threaten to complain when their requests couldn't be immediately met. They are abusive and physical when this causes standard drinks to come late.

They walk about to examine cabin features and look for family and friends. Everyone badgers for something to take. The amenities containers are soon empty, and the men quite drunk. Though most passengers ordered special meals; when the meal service begins, they want something else. Interruptions and demands continue, and dinner drags on till we land.

The nightmare continues on ground when wheelchairs have to be provided not only for fat and old people, but strong and fit-looking men as well. The passengers leave, and gangs of hungry staff board the plane to prepare its return. The scrawny men pester us for drinks and gifts, and their eyes dart everywhere for stuff to steal. It's normal for five or six cleaners to surround a small patch of rubbish with brooms and other cleaning paraphernalia, but none doing anything.

***

After waiting about forty-five minutes, this time, for high-handed, haughty officials, we make our way out of the dingy, mosquito inhabited airport. In spite of the ostentatious poverty and monsoon in the richest city of this famished country where the immensely rich live beyond the reach of most people, I am immensely relieved. I'm getting a respite for seven days, away from worldly trials and tribulations.

We leave customs and reach a dim area where desperate faces sit on the top of craned necks to wait behind rusty railings. A few dark empty restaurants later, we leave the terminal and walk uneasily on darker pavements. Empty black-and-yellow taxis and three-wheeled toot-toots fill the road, their drivers beseeching us to board. Stepping gingerly over puddles of filthy water, we follow the guide past rows of people with hands outstretched. They tug at our clothes persistently or try to pull pens off our pockets, as a noisome smell hangs over the stifling, damp atmosphere.

Frail porters with long thin arms lug our heavy luggage onto the top of a drab medium-sized bus. We climb rickety steps, positioned for us, to board.

The smell of insecticide in the cabin overwhelms us as a hundred oversize mosquitoes sink and float in greeting. Slow and careless, since they're drunk and overfed, they knock our squeamish faces and buzz at our ears. Everyone has a sunken seat to rest our weary bodies on. It is dirty and torn, with a headrest cover (black where the head is) and most likely, a broken armrest. The fans above the seats swirl back and forth near our ears, as damp grungy curtains stroke frustrated faces and tousle hair. The men heave the excess bags onto the aisle, and the shy guide waves goodbye.

The helper slams the door shut. He bends, enters the spacious driver's compartment and closes its panel door behind him. The bus trundles off into the shadows of the decrepit city, with the mosquitoes forced into retreat.

***

Now I can resume thinking from where I stopped. During service on board, I had told myself, it was truly a temporary interruption. It wasn't easy to accept it, though I succeeded.

I'm lucky to have two seats. I place my jacket on the vacant seat beside me, pull the curtain open and strap it to one side of the filthy glass window. The sullen crew looks depressed as the bus meanders round potholes and unknown objects on the dimly lit road. It rolls, picks up speed and shakes to the cacophony of slithering music, blaring honks and sputtering engines. It splashes muddy water at passing vehicles and pedestrians walking on the sides.

Huge, dully coloured billboards flaunting elegant English remind me of London countryside roads after Heathrow Airport. At lower levels, are black-and-white posters with serious faces of candidates from different political parties. Lights dot the moonlit darkness to the horizon as rows of tattered tents appear on fields.

Ravens and crows sweep the night, cawing bitterly; or perch on overhanging, crisscrossing cables croaking with complaints. The bus passes lines of black bodies covered with dark cloths, sleeping on concrete parapets and pavements. Men with backs towards us, trousers or *dhotis* pulled down from the waist in front, stand here and there to urinate.

The cabin comes alive as some crew members shift and pull the grimy curtains gingerly. As their heads peer out, whispers of alarm are followed, to my disbelief, with bursts of sniggers and derogatory remarks.

I stare at the immediate darkness in front of me, and try to think. I don't want distraction, but I keep looking out of the glass at my side like the others. I tell myself we would be in the comfort and safety of our bus for at least one hour and twenty-five minutes, and I would be free of work and responsibilities for many days. Later on, I would be sheltered in the most luxurious hotel in the vast country. If I don't want to leave my room for food, room service is cheap and available at the lift of a handset. I expect to be comforted by this thought, but it doesn't seem to take me. I repeat the thought in my head a few more times, but it doesn't help. The lack of comfort now would all right, I tell myself, if I could complete thinking.

I remind myself to appreciate I won't be disturbed, once I'm in my room in this country which could give me insights. At the end of this stay, perhaps I would find the answers I've been seeking for so long, if I am disciplined and try hard enough. But I'm not sure what to do. Besides, my past experience in the country tells me not to be sanguine.

I like the world outside. At the same time, I am even more afraid of it. It always crept upon me and pricked the very bubble it helped me build. My bubble is neither spiritual nor opulent. It is plain and normal – and even dull. But I prize it even when calling it a bubble. Once pricked, it bursts, and reorientation is impossible. I would be in pieces and can't be put together for some time. I hope it's all right here. There is little in the world to lose here, so I'm less worried about the bubble. The world stays quite where it is, so long as I stay out of trouble.

I've still not resumed thinking from where I should start. I'm very disappointed with myself. I put up mental shutters to keep out the feeling, but it continues to peer at me now and then.

The driver swerves to avoid a tall elephantine bus filled with gaudy colours. It moves slowly, weighed down by objects that jut out on all sides.

Passengers sit or stand inside like packed sardines while others hang outside like fishes from hooks. Others squat with luggage on top of the swaying vehicle and gawk at us looking at them from our bus. The drivers of both buses horn, crane out their necks and curse each other above the din of the road. As our bus veers to the left, the other vehicle dances in the same direction. The distance in between stays the same because of the jutting passengers.

We pass more lines of sleeping bodies and tattered tents. Scrawny, diseased mongrels nose the ground for scraps of food. They lift one hind leg to urinate or squat on both to defecate.

More travelling later, the driver honks impatiently and the bus crawls on an empty road. People lie on both sides like corpses. Two large cows with protruding ribs and hips, trot lazily out of our way before a tiny roundabout. They stop; long, desiccated udders swinging, to drop damp substances reflecting the moonlight. The lumps on the floor, they disappear and a dung stench fills our cabin.

The rascals made a point, the crew stir and pass snide remarks. They pinch their noses and snigger. The bus manoeuvres slowly around more clods of dung with tyre marks. Inside the private compartment, the driver curses, his assistant chatters, as both men wriggle and shake their heads. Their vibrating mouths open and shut like machines.

All of a sudden, the movements stop. Three lanky men in khaki uniform, holding long *lathi* sticks, appear on the roadside. They hurl long runny sentences at the driver – for hogging the road. The bus stops, making everyone worried. The helper enters the cabin. The lights blink and brighten slowly like a pampered cow opening its lazy eyes.

A policeman boards the bus uncertainly. Above his long body, the bewildered eyes blink and stare. The face breaks into a big grin when they see the hostesses. A drowsy mosquito rises, and the head jerks back. The body straightens suddenly, a knee overshoots upwards, and a foot stamps hard. A loud crash follows, and the floor shakes. A long arm creeps carefully, and the hand gives the girl in front a salute.

He turns slowly and goes carefully down the dim steps. The bus is freed with a jerk. Murmurs of relief are heard when the captain congratulates the hostess for the smile which solved everything.

The turbaned policeman with long curly whiskers beat the bus away with his long lathi. The bus squashes more mounds, then jolts when a front wheel falls into a pothole. It shakes again as its rear wheel hits the same pothole.

I adjust the digital face of my Casio against the dim street lights outside, repeatedly, to see the time. We are on the road for about half an hour, yet we've not travelled far. It is another hour before we reach the hotel, by the famous arch on the Apollo Bunder waterfront where all sorts of activities take place. A flash in my mind tells how dogs feel if there is food to last a long time. I tell myself I still have time.

I recline my seat in satisfaction, making sure the knees behind me aren't hurt. I'm going to continue thinking in earnest. I mustn't waste time; I have been too relaxed. To my dismay, I remember vividly the last time I was in this city on my way home from London.

I wanted to pass my one-day stay quickly. I had hoped I wouldn't have a care in this so-called spiritual country. All I wanted was to see the fortune teller since he was very detailed and accurate. His presence was overwhelming, I was told. He was a clairvoyant and could see deep inside a person's mind. I wanted to know whether all this was true. Perhaps, he was the man who could free my mind. Twenty American dollars would be worth spending.

***

After that flight and I checked in: once I woke up, I went to his office in the hotel to book an appointment. I was disappointed the smartly-dressed, fair-skinned man was available straightaway. I was even more dismayed he looked professional. The well-lit, air-conditioned office appeared like a modern small library. A small altar sat at its entrance with the strong smell of incense. Erudite looking English books filled up tall shelves around the room.

I sat opposite the middle-aged, bespectacled man – a large, spanking blue turban hugging his head, behind the oak desk. Two framed diagrams with English explanations, one with a human face drawn, the other a palm, hung on the wall above my own head.

"Good sir, what are you doing in my country?"
He spoke clear grammatical English as he looked at
me with probing eyes.

"I work as a flight steward."

"Oh, you're from that airline. Am I right? It's the
greatest in the world. Whenever I travel, I always
fly your airline, if it goes to where I am going, that
is. Please believe me, I'm not lying. What do you
like to do when you are not working?"

"I think a lot. I worry about who I am. I read. I
swim."

"Let me see your palm."

I showed him.

"How long has your good self been in this
wonderful airline? May I ask what your esteemed
rank is?"

That was when I had to find out whether people
who claimed to have supernatural power were
fakes. Was he gathering information, so he could
pretend to know my past and future?

"Twelve years," I told him suspiciously. "I'm an
Assistant Purser. I was promoted not long ago."

"Are you happy with your job?"

I didn't feel like answering his questions
anymore.

"It's a very good job," he continued. He
wriggled his head and stopped. "How many siblings
do you have?"

I couldn't stop myself from answering. "One
brother, five sisters."

Then I began to think I shouldn't miss any of his
words.

"And how are you placed in the family, kind sir?"

"I'm the youngest male. Third youngest in the family."

He continued to look at me with searching eyes.

"I see your past and your future. You left the army before you joined the airline. You didn't like life in the army. Your family looks after you. Tell me if I am wrong." He is still watching my face as I nodded. "Let me say this. You've had your promotions. But from now on, your climb will be arduous."

"What should I do to be happy? That is all I care for."

He touched the sides of my face with the tips of his soft fingers, scrutinising my eyes.

"You've a lot of nervous energy. If you use it in the right way, you will benefit. If not, it will destroy you."

"Did you say I have a lot of nervous energy?"

"Behold, your face tells me everything."

"Can you tell me whether I would be successful in life?"

"It all depends on you. It's my duty not to tell too much. All I'm allowed to say is that if you channel your energy in the correct manner, you will be successful. Success is yours if you do what is right."

Then he had looked at me blankly, and I knew the twenty US dollar session was over. I left with the strong feeling I was cheated. I began thinking I should have probed the eloquent man with pointed questions, mercilessly.

I realised it isn't true I wouldn't have a care in the world under certain circumstances. If I didn't find anything in this case, I would've wasted my time. If I missed something, I couldn't find the whole truth. I didn't mind losing the money, as I thought the experience was in fact worthwhile.

Still, I can't give up the notion I can move around in this "holy" country without a care.

***

We pass pitched black shantytowns, fronted with food and drink stalls, sheltered under grimy *Thums Up* parasols, and political banners like "Vote Congress Party". A stretch of pastel beach with a row of dull lights appears in the distance. Though it looks lacking, it has the shape of an arc and increasingly, the impression of a necklace dotted with jewels. This must be Marine Drive, I tell myself to believe: the Queen's necklace as they love to call it. It looks like the Victoria Necklace locals like to talk about, out of pride their Head of State was once a British monarch.

This has to be it! How many beaches can there be in a city! Then I realise I'm wrong as there is water between the land the bus is driving on and that piece of matter which looks like a beach. A lagoon should be there whereas Marine Drive is a normal beach. I must be wary of wrong conclusions! I must be alert in order not to accept wrong teachings! It's too easy to believe in something. This is how people get carried further and further from the truth.

That fortune teller wanted me to believe he knew, through supernatural means, I left the army. But he knew every male from the island becomes a soldier at eighteen. He also knew I was from the Airline, and openings were no longer aplenty. He took a calculated risk with his prediction.

Now I sit up straight and look for more signs the grey patch is water. *It is not. It is.* It's flat (do I see waves on the patch?), located below a darker piece of undulating substance tinged with different colours. No other signs on the distant object, except the lights which I look in between for signs of life and buildings. If I can see buildings, this piece of land could be Marine Drive. I'm not sure how to conceive the lights. In fact, they are mere circles of vagueness, each circle becoming vaguer before it joins another piece of vagueness.

I fall into paralysis, worrying if it is Marine Bay, yet trying not to have a care on my shoulders in this supposedly religious country. One in the morning, 3.30 a.m where I am from: I'm extremely sleepy but not allowing myself to fall asleep, I feel like a dying man who can't die because he refuses to let go.

I say to myself: *at least, I have done some thinking.* Eventually, the bus will trundle onto the roads in the heart of this fascinating city, and I would have to accept that one chapter ends the way it is (whether I like it or not) again, and another chapter begins without mercy. I want very badly to go any way I want to go – or I am led – but I'm not able to write off my feelings.

***

An underfed fortysomething with a blue JTB badge hanging from his breast pocket – on the cobblestoned pavement at the Gateway of India – looms out of the chaos of my tortured mind. All that happened that day in *the heart of the city* comes in a flash.

I had stepped off the small motorised boat and walked through the grimy asphalt arch, away from shaken fellow passengers. They had either clung on helplessly or threw out sea water with anything, after sudden strong waves nearly capsized the overloaded boat on my return from Elephanta Caves. He stood in the hot afternoon sun – hair unkempt, grinning widely – exposing rust-coloured, betel-nut-stained teeth as he waited for me to reach him. His wrinkled shirt was outside the waist of unwashed dark trousers.

"Are you Japanese or Chinese? *Ohayou gozaimasu, ni hao ma?* I know Japanese and Chinese." He spoke English with the twist. "I am Professor Devanas, history department, University of Delhi. Why you take the boat?"

"We almost died."

"You shouldn't travel on your own here. You need guide. I'm from Japan Tourist Bureau."

"I like travelling on my own."

The crowds, made up of mostly men dressed like Devanas amble on the smelly promenade. Among them were sweaty bodies wrapped with *dhotis* from the waist down, women in colourful saris exposing stacks of flabby waists, and old British tourists in hats and hot jackets. They were keenly watched by cripples crawling on the uneven ground and beggars, fortune tellers with fat little birds in wooden cages, hawkers selling anything from balloons to flimsy pin-ball toys, and altars with lighted, fragrant incense. Charmers blew music snaking out of bulbous flutes amid the incessant noise as cobras twisted gracefully up and down. The snakes curled docilely into lidded rattan baskets after the ostentatious display. A bearded *sadhu* with long matted hair, his face painted white and yellow, walked by confidently in an orange robe. Weird trinkets stringed from an overloaded neck. Tourists snapped photographs with childlike enthusiasm. Foreigners aimed cameras at bizarre or unflattering scenes as proud locals stared disdainfully and complained at the disrespect amongst themselves.

A scrawny, shirtless boy with dead eyes and a stomach like a full-blown balloon, stood in front of us, stretching his grimy hand. Gluey green snot lengthening from one nostril and licked at his lips, retreated each time he sniffed. Devanas, following behind, pulled me by my elbow as I was giving the boy some rupees while an expressionless man in white with a Gandhi *topi* on his head, watched.

"No, no. Don't give!" Devanas grunted and shook his index finger at the boy. The beggar's opaque eyes looked at Devanas' hard ones, before the bare body disappeared into the crowd. "Let me bring you see. Every morning, big boss brings children to Shivaji Park. He gives child one piece *puri* and little curry, and one drink water and sends them out. In the evening, they come back same place to give money. If he gets much money, he gives everyone one, two rupees. If children have no money or little money, he beats them. Children were taken by "mafia" and police when young. Doctors cut off hands and legs so people pity them. You give one, many many come. ... I show you Shivaji Park. Nearby."

A black muscular man with red veiny eyes crept up on lean buttocks, brandishing a dirty bowl in one misshapen hand. Only rounded stumps were left on his knees. His brown singlet (once white) and tattered shorts were covered with dirt. There was helpless anger and a pitiless acceptance of his cruel fate on his stone-hard eyes. He could be suffering since being seized as a boy. He saw Devanas. Without a second look, he scuttled like a crab away.

I couldn't breathe in the giddying stench of urine. A barefooted boy with an open satchel full of Archie comics, showed me a copy with misspelled, ungrammatical English. Devanas slapped the little head a few times and shrieked.

"Get lost! Don't disturb tourist!"

The pale face winced and disappeared. I tried to walk away from Devanas, but it was too crowded. He followed me past blots of trampled red spittle on the floor, gasping behind.

"Let me bring you. This place not safe. I repeat, not safe."

I turned around. "Don't follow me!"

A few men nearly walked into me again, and adroitly turned away. A dusty boy with a talisman hanging from his neck and lines of sweat on his bare chest, tugged my shirt weakly and whispered a few rupees could buy a woman of my choice. Then a hawker appeared and wanted me to buy the catapults in his hand. I bought one, and he insisted I buy another at a reduced price. Devanas gave me a vindicated look and strutted away.

A barefooted teenage mother with a savvy face, holding a naked child within the crook of her arm on one side of her waist, walked stealthily towards me. The free hand clutched an empty baby bottle, and her impish eyes watched Devanas with hate, as he moved further away. The light on the child's vacuous eyes was fading. Nearby, the wall was splashed with bright colours. Below the colours, the wall and the floor were wet with urine.

I walked quickly towards Apollo Bunder Road, twisting my wet body into any small hole which opened among the bodies. I try to breathe less till I was free of the crowd, but there was no respite. In front of the stone embankment, by the chaotic roar and pollution of crisscrossing traffic, away from the grey sea of floating rubbish and occasional faeces, a man squatted. His bare hands were holding the pants at his knees, as he talked to himself. There was nothing to wipe his exposed bottom with. He looked at me blankly, then stared at someone approaching.

Devanas was laughing and cursing, pointing at him. The man stared at the badge on Devanas' shirt, got up immediately, and his back bent as he tried to pull up his trousers – ran. It was magic: the badge caused fear. That was why Devanas wore it all the time. And he chose a foreign sounding one from a rich country with its aura of prestige.

I crossed the cracked, worn tarmac full of holes and solitary stones, and stepped onto the dirt-filled pavement. It was cluttered with rubbish and congested with dirty bicycles and blackened pedestrians. People sat or squatted on the bare floor with empty eyes, as if waiting for their turn to die.

A small tricycle stall with no customers, offered deep-fried pancakes languishing beside a pot of cold black oil. Flies took off the dry, shrivelled food with each sweep of the vendor's hand and landed again. Finally, the skinny hand crept to the handle of the long flyswatter at the side. The plastic grating rose, stayed still for a while and came down hard. The unpitied creature rose too late and joined numerous mortally flattened dots on the floor.

I liked the sweet milky *chai* from these stalls, which I obsessively drank. I had to feel the city; and the tea was safe if I was sure it was hot.

But I was stopped by a bare-footed boy with a shoe brush and a tin of polish in his hands, insisting on the right to shine my sneakers. Next to him, stood the teenage mother with her naked child. She watched us, as its head swayed lifelessly against the crook of her arm. Some pushing and pulling later, I broke free of the shoeshiner's hands. I dashed through the side door into the huge building in front, and the guard blocked the boy.

Guilt and confusion hit me as I asked if I should have done something for the dying child. I took the lift to my cold floor and walked quickly on the stained, creased carpet to escape the strong insecticide smell. I entered my room and chained the door. I laid a piece of paper on my desk and recorded all my day's experiences on it, entitled: *A Cacophony of Noise, Smells and Activities*. I had found it necessary not to lose anything I experienced and learnt.

Beyond the glass doors, on the dusty, smoggy balcony in one of the favourite haunts of maharajahs, the crows were quarrelling. It was a day well-spent.

***

I recover from the reverie. The bus turns down, bumping slowly on a dark road lined on both sides with colonial buildings. The city is recharging for a new day, after frenetic activities.

People are awake at this unearthly hour: lost souls who can't rest while the country sleeps soundly, who are helpless like insomniac crew members. These people live outside the mainstream of society, move quietly and cast wary looks. They see weary bodies lying with their children, sheltered on covered pavements in front of indented buildings, full of the stench of urine and clogged open drains. They see human scavengers pick through rubbish in search of stuff to reuse or eat, while rodents squeak outside pretentious restaurants and do the same. They see fat cats prowl silently, waiting for the right moment to pounce on deserving well-fed prey. Lone souls living on quiet moments of the city, sleeping when it awakes in a few hours. They're witnesses of another world, souls who pray for unconsciousness when madness in the world begins.

And I've already withdrawn into myself as I found myself doing anywhere. I become afraid like I was anywhere. I hide in familiarity. Which is the reason Devanas' blue badge always hangs on his breast. That was why I was in my world that day. That was why I was thinking and doing things the same way.

That is the reason change is so difficult. Perhaps, that is why I'm still in the airline. It seems to me, at this moment, my set of crew is the luckiest people in the world. We are taking leave of pain and reality. My leave hasn't even started, yet I'm already free. I don't think I should believe all that.

"*Babu!*" someone shouts from afar. I hear clippity-clop approaching, slowing down and a haggard scruffy horse pulling a big carriage appears. It neighs weakly. The bus stops. Mosquitoes wake up and hover before me. My fingers strain to slide open the translucent pane. The moonlit night is bright, once the glass is pushed aside. A stench of stale water and dried urine lingers in the still, damp air.

"Me am Ali and let me bring anywhere in this city on my 'Victoria' slowly see city sights as you relax like kings and queens, anytime in my cart which is an original of England." The hideous eyes and a twitching nose approach the open window. The hand raises the bottle to the mouth which drinks the whisky like water.

The grimy coachman towers above me on the raised driver's seat. His free hand waves at me and points in the direction of the musty smell coming from the calash. Both wide front- facing and narrow back-facing seats are covered with torn upholstery. A tattered folded top flops behind the back seat. Bags of beers and stuff hang on both sides of the old malnourished animal. The sleep deprived, tired horse wobbles to the floor. A lash flies from a hand onto its bony back. It stands unsteadily, protesting with another whine.

"If you propose two horses, you only pay two. I've som'ore horses in my big stable nearby. No? You going away? I wait for you outside hotel tomorrow. Bring friends, as many if possible, same price and you'll not regret because I know many about this wonderful city." The bus departs, chugging louder and louder in the quiet of the night as it picks up speed.

An hour has consciously slipped by beyond my control. It's time to end this chapter. In about a minute, I will pass the celebrated arch.

Chapter 12
The Crucifixion of Feng

I've searched the entire estate for Feng but couldn't find him. He was not at the library where he normally did research each time he returned home from a flight. I even called his family. They got worried, of course, but I know Feng would be able to handle all this. I only wanted to console him. He must be wandering in confusion, all by himself, weighed down by hurt and anger, unable to do what he feels he should be doing. There would be mountains of worries. He couldn't fly anymore. He has given up the job he loves, the security and certainty it afforded him, and all the women who love him. There would be no turning back.

The foundation on which his world was built has collapsed. His love of life based on the worth of mankind is shaken to the core. He would understand, now, it had just been a desperate attempt by himself to find its meaning. This heavy burden may weigh on his shoulders for the rest of his life, during which he will wonder if he would ever find something else again. His body may feel collapsed and his legs giving way. His mind would be swimming, and he won't know what to do.

He will be trying to come to terms with all this. I don't want him to change his mind and regret. That is close to impossible for him. Moreover, he is capable of achieving more in life than pandering to the whims of passengers in the airline which suits only mediocre bums – and lost souls like me.

I was waiting for this to happen, anyway. I knew he would eventually find himself humiliated and betrayed. His love and optimism of the world was extreme. He never held back when someone needed help or asked for it. He was always prepared to forgive in spite of occasional acts of tough love.

He was getting too involved in the problems of Howard and Connie. I told him before, not to spend too much time on them, but he wouldn't listen. They were both adults, and they got themselves into this mess. Not that he hadn't helped them, but they've let it drag on too long. At the end, it is their own problem and they've to sort it out themselves. He has his own priorities to get back to.

When Howard told Connie to leave him (on Feng's advice), she had agreed to do so. Her Ward Leader who was interested in Connie from the day she joined the airline, learnt about it and began to court her. The trouble started when Howard told the other girl to leave him as well, and Connie came to know about it. She had hoped to get back to Howard and as a matter of principle, refused to meet the Cabin Crew Executive (CCE) again. Howard and Connie already developed feelings for each other, and they trusted each other. They seemed to be made for each other. The CCE was furious. Connie was confused over what to do. Howard, as usual generous, was willing to give way to her Ward Leader. But when Howard's lover committed suicide and he was suspected of killing her, Connie asked Feng for advice and Feng had said she had every right to do what she wished. Feng's argument was that Connie and the CCE were mere friends. Unfortunately, the CCE is not an ordinary crew member since the director of the department is his brother-in-law. The Ward Leader kept up the pressure on her. She and Howard found themselves in different parts of the world all the time. She found crew members picking on her, and letters of complaints started to come in. She suspected the CCE was behind all this and asked Feng to help. That was how the CCE came to regard Feng as his bitter enemy.

The past few days make me feel that I had done my part, but I'm not sure. A part of me as usual, had held back. Those events are still very clear. They keep reappearing in my mind, and I can't think of anything else.

***

It happened four days ago, when I was called up to replace another AP who reported sick at the last minute.

I had walked into the briefing room at the control centre and closed the door. The tubby, bald Purser with long arms and hairy hands I recognised straightaway as Eric Oliveiro, was seated in front of a broken table which was still usable. He was facing seventeen crew members on damaged chairs in a U-shape in front of him. The other AP happened to be Feng. Both of us were promoted to the rank some time ago. Connie was also on the flight. She now a JP in a green floral *sarong kebaya.* I only realised why the crew looked so serious and tense when I saw a CCE sitting next to her. Eric spoke nervously as he tried to be his jovial self. Then he handed the briefing over to the CCE.

The CCE spoke slowly, somewhat mumbling. "I expect everyone to live by company's requirements whenever you are on its time. Standards must always be kept. Senior crew must always be exemplary. This is especially true of APs because when the Purser is not around, he becomes the Crew-in-Charge."

Eric's simian mouth seemed to try not to burst a bubble inside, the two lips shifting in and out, carefully, like mechanised plates as he calmed himself. "Mr Richard Phang is our Ward Leader. Most of us belong to his team. If you're from other teams, remember you're still part of the crew operating this flight. I assume everyone has met Mr Phang by now."

There was heavy silence.

Richard was tall and had a handsome face, but he slouched and was obviously in need of exercise. He adjusted the reading glasses on top of his knobby nose and looked above the frame at Feng with knitted brows. "Feng, you're an AP. Do you think you have set a good example? Did you introduce yourself to me?"

"I met you before, Mr Phang," Feng said coolly. "So it wasn't necessary for me to shake your hand again. I did look at you and you smiled at me outside, before we came into the room."

"That's the problem with you crew," Eric said, grinning nervously. "You people like to argue, but you don't use your brains. Do you know when you talk back like that, it's insubordination? Look at your last three fingers when the index points at someone. Don't they point back more?"

I never met Richard before, and had forgotten to introduce myself to him. The junior crew also didn't introduce themselves to me. I wanted to bring this up, but it would surely bring trouble to rest of the crew and me.

Richard continued. "I want all of you to watch your appearance. There have been many complaints from passengers that crew were not smiling these days. This is going to be a long and tiring night. Keep yourselves well-groomed and fresh throughout. Watch out if your breath stinks. Remember: passengers' breaths can smell as much as they like but not yours. And if you have something to say that the Purser should know, make sure he know. Don't cover up each other's mistakes. Let me know what you told Eric after that. By the way, I want to show you good grooming by picking someone in this room. Look at Connie. She is the epitome of our hostesses. She smells good. Her hair is neat and her makeup perfect. There is friendliness and warmth on her face, and she always has a pleasant smile. Her appearance conforms to Company's standards. She is exemplary in behavior too." Connie looking embarrassed, stared at her mermaid lap wrapped in the fitting sarong.

When the briefing was over, the crew left quietly for the departure hall. Richard took Connie's bag and put it on top of his on his luggage trolley. He pulled the trolley and Connie followed sullenly. That was when I realised Richard was the very man

Connie was trying to avoid, the man known to be very harsh to guys.

Richard is a divorcee obsessively biased towards hostesses, especially if they were young and pretty. Junior stewards who greeted him told me horror stories how they were snubbed. Richard drives an old Jaguar. I was sure Feng was his target on this flight.

The hunched, gangly figure pulled the burden, waddled through the departure hall and cleared Immigration. Beautiful and elegant Connie was on his left while Eric, his bag hanging from his long arm, was on his right. Richard bent low to adjust Connie's bag so it wouldn't slide further to one side. Trailing were a hostess and a steward looking important. I caught up with the group.

"Liu," Eric said, maintaining his American accent. "I need a favour from you. We've to help the Company watch Feng. There were complaints from passengers and staff about him. If any of you see him do something wrong, let Richard and I know." He turned to the two crew members behind. "Especially the two of you working with him."

"You want the report straightaway or after the flight?" the athlete-looking steward asked earnestly.

"See for yourself whether it's urgent," Richard said. "If the matter can't wait, let us know immediately. Leave the service, if you must. Otherwise, let us know when convenient. But do it before the end of this flight. It is common sense."

"All of you, listen," Eric said. "Keep this within ourselves."

I flew with Eric before. Then he was one of the kindest and most helpful pursers I had met. But tonight, he was dangerous because Richard was checking his flight. I looked at Connie's peach-shaped face which had turned white. I felt sorry for her. I was determined to scupper the trap laid out for Feng. I stood still on the travelator and let the clique walk away.

**

I heard purposeful steps catching up and then Feng's cheerful voice.

"How're you, Liu?" He stopped walking on the travelator too as it continued to slide towards the gate hold room.

"Good." I used to say that whether or not I was fine. "Be careful of the steward and hostess working with you."

"Don't worry about them. I am a free man."

"They are spies."

I told him quickly what happened. I didn't tell him to keep this a secret, as I knew he would do what had to be done. He didn't seem to worry.

"I've done nothing wrong. Why should I be afraid?"

We came near the gate. Passengers were waiting for the glass doors to open. The pilots were already standing there. Richard was speaking to the Captain, the darkness in his eyes saying he was talking bad about Feng. Eric spoke excitedly to crew members gathered around him. He moved agilely, smiling and joking.

We slid off the travelator and stepped onto the soft carpet. Connie waited for us to pass her before throwing me a whisper: "Tell Feng, be careful!"

I smiled without looking at her. I had learnt to smile when I had to, not when I meant it. It's part of my job. We walked through the gate which just opened.

Feng placed his pilot case flat on the security belt and walked through the metal detector. I was about to do the same when I felt Gopal behind me. I could see his movements, as his neck arched over my shoulder, and he glanced at the greenish screen. He was deciphering the X-ray patterns in Feng's case inside the machine. He looked at Richard and Eric, hoping to see that they notice what he was doing. They weren't looking, and he hid his disappointment. He laid his bag on the belt and followed me through the detector. He slunk behind me as I walked towards Feng.

"What are you guys doing in Melbourne?" Gopal asked when we were together. Feng and I ignored his presence which was nervous and arrogant. Gopal continued, "Shall we drink in my room? Should I carry something from the bar?"

I pulled Feng away from him. "Gopal was finding out if we're taking stuff from the aircraft."

Gopal looked at me suspiciously, his prominent features making him look sinister. We left him and walked on the aerobridge into the huge, brightly lit B747 cabin.

***

It was already a beehive of activity with cleaners and caterers scurrying about, artisans lying on the floor as they checked this and that. I walked to door 2 right where my crew seat was located to check the safety equipment. I had to make sure they were there and in working condition. Feng trotted up the staircase to the Stamford Class in the upper deck where he was in charge. Gopal strutted up after him, followed by the hostess. One after another, the rest of the crew entered the cabin with grim faces. They stowed their belongings and began to work.

I took the meal breakdown from the Galley Hostess in my section of the Stamford class (in the main deck) on a piece of paper and gave it to Eric. He snatched and pushed it into one of his trouser pockets. He walked over to the tape recorder mounted on the wall forward of door 2 left and removed the cassette. He looked at it, then slotted it back. He pressed the start button, the rewind button and the start button again. The announcement for the safety demonstration came on shortly. I raised my thumb at Eric to let him know the announcement in my area was loud and clear. Feng and the rest of the complex leaders did the same from their respective zones.

Richard walked to Eric and stared up the staircase at the upper deck galley. He bent to whisper into Eric's ear. "Has he done it?"

But Eric was bending over a small greyish smudge on the wall, just aft of door 2 left.

"Liu," Eric said loudly in a singing tone. "Come here. Didn't you see this?" He stabbed repeatedly at the stain when I got there. "Get a floor cloth and wipe this away?"

I went to the galley and returned with the cloth.

"You are very alert. Good job," Richard said to Eric. "Has Feng reported on the announcement?"

"You've to be alert when you are a Purser, Richard. Thanks for the compliment anyway. Oh yes, he has reported."

Richard nodded sullenly and straightened his droopy back. I pushed open the bifold toilet door and wet the cloth under the tap. As I pressed liquid soap from the bottle dispenser onto the damp part of the cloth, Feng came down and handed Eric his meal breakdown. Eric took the paper and examined it closely. I rubbed the soapy cloth, to and fro, on the stain.

Eric smirked as he said to Feng. "Total number of trays added up correctly; the numbers of each type of meals and the special meals, all added nicely; bar numbers given. Very good!" He flicked the piece of paper up and down. "Where is the number of towels? Where are the different types of newspapers?"

Feng looked at Eric curiously: "I have been doing this every flight. I think everyone does it."

"Aha! Every Purser has his style. Some are good leaders, some are lousy. Some are *bo chap* and couldn't be bothered."

"I didn't know your style."

"You have to find out. How long have you been an AP?"

"But ..."

"Shut up!" Richard snapped, sounding hysterical. Saliva spattered onto Feng's face. "Feng, respect your Purser. You are a bad example for the crew. You question your superior in their presence. I want to see a change in you immediately."

The atmosphere was now one of undisguised intimidation. The heavily tattooed catering officer with long hair and an earring looked at the dressing down impassively, as he pushed the trolley loaded with containers into my galley. The crew checking the service buttons and opening the air vents in the forward part of the cabin, worked silently with anxious eyes. Connie holding a canister of freshener peeked nervously from the First Class as she entered the toilet and closed the door. I thought: *Richard, Feng has shown respect! He kept quiet when your stinking saliva spattered onto his face.*

A sense of injustice arose in me. I walked up to Richard, the floor cloth dangling from my hand and looked at his face coldly. I could see the red veins and the pulsating sclera on his inflamed eyes. I was going to give him a piece of my mind when the three pilots walked into the cabin, and the Captain spoke to him. Together the four men climbed the steps to the upper deck.

I was again rubbing the damp cloth against the stain though I knew now it couldn't be removed with soap and water. Nearby, the engineer bent over a cushionless seat, dripping with sweat, as he worked with kneeling artisans. He wouldn't have enough time to remove the stain before take-off.

I could see Richard, Gopal and the three pilots in the galley upstairs from here. The pilots were looking at menu cards while the steward waited with a piece of paper. They were deciding what to eat from the three classes after take-off, and what to drink on ground. Then they turned around for the cockpit in front of the upper deck cabin.

"Thanks in advance for a good flight," I heard Richard fawn after them.

He hung his languid arm on Gopal's shoulder. The two men are about the same height. He said authoritatively, "Look after the pilots well. Remind Feng they are having soup and satay. And to get them caviar if it is available."

"Yes sir," Gopal said with a show of enthusiasm. "I'm sure we will make it for the breakfast allowance."

The hostess brought some used glasses she found in the cabin. She smiled at Richard coquettishly.

"How is Feng doing?" Richard asked her gently.

"He's all right. He's doing his work, don't worry. I'll let you know if anything is wrong."

Richard walked into the cabin with his soft hands clasped behind his hips – to watch Feng work, I supposed. The steward and the hostess are in a celebratory mood. As Gopal made her a drink, she opened the dry store cart to search for packets of nuts.

I walked quickly to the First Class to look for the Cabin Defects Log book. Connie found the worn out book in the ship's bag and recorded the stain for me. She was tensed up and unhappy.

I returned to the Stamford Class in time to see upstairs, Richard walk into the galley and Feng follow. Richard's face looked irritated when he turned around and confronted Feng, but he was laughing too. I pretended to examine the service console above the seat at where I was standing, as though to check on the hostess' work. From here, I continue to watch what was happening in the upper deck galley.

"I can't understand," Richard said condescendingly. "The pilots were here, but it was the galley steward who greeted them and took their orders. Where were you as the complex leader? Were you in the toilet, taking your sweet time to comb your hair?"

Feng didn't answer. He looked at Richard steadily. Without a word, he turned around and walked out of the galley.

We were all very busy after that, except for Eric and Richard. Passengers began to board. Richard stood there (in main deck Stamford Class) for some time and stared at me impassively.

***

After take-off, bouts of turbulence during the drinks and dinner services were accompanied by jarring, crackling announcements that the no-smoking signs were switched on. The crew rushed to the toilets and knocked on the doors to inform passengers to return to their seats. They walked up and down the aisles, to remind them to have their seat belts fastened. They made parents remove their infants from the bassinets.

Gopal passed my zone on his way to the First Class several times during the services. It is normal to look for stuff passengers and the pilots needed which were available only in First Class, except he had been there too often. I could imagine him talking to Eric about Feng; even adding salt and pepper to suit his taste. I looked at him with disgust each time he returned, and he returned me with an arrogant stare.

The cabin light was switched off after dinner, and I sat on the crew seat facing the toilet at door 2 left. Alone and undisturbed in the dark, the events of the night leading to the now, flashed through my mind. I saw a path to this "location" in space and time, in which I glimpsed everything that happened. But once I saw everything, I realised I hadn't seen everything. I looked again and saw everything before me and I didn't see it again. I stopped this thought process because I knew I could never complete it without disruptions.

I walked slowly on the aisle to the First Class cabin. All was dark and quiet. There were only two passengers, who were sleeping, although Stamford and Value classes were both full. It was normal on this route.

Connie was chatting with the other JP in the dimmed galley. They sat on metal containers they had carried down from the compartments. The folded blankets laid on the cold metal softened the uneven surfaces and handles.

Eric and Richard were sleeping without jackets. Each one was slumped on a First Class seat although the crew was not allowed to lie or sit on First Class and Stamford seats. They were also not supposed to rest because the flight time was less than eleven hours. Richard looked pitiful like a very tired old man. His flabby face was very haggard. I knew once he refreshed himself, he would be hounding his victims mercilessly. I couldn't really blame him when he was paid to do his job.

I reminded myself not to agonise over the pains of people. No amount of feeling on my part would make it less painful for them. Everyone lives alone whether they know it or not. Feng would've to realise he was no exception. He would've to accept that his ideas about humanity and the warmth it provides were lies made for people like him.

I couldn't let myself be trapped by thoughts on this flight. I turned to return to my zone. Connie was waiting in front of the curtain between the bulkheads for me.

"Liu," she whispered as I lowered my ear. "That idiot, Richard, turned Captain against Feng. Captain came to find Richard, but he was sleeping. Good luck: Captain then told me what he was going to tell Richard. He said Feng only gave him food and drinks. There was no service. He even had to remind Feng to get the caviar."

"What service does he expect?" I blurted, keeping my voice down. "We're all colleagues. We don't give pilots service. We only serve passengers. When the load is light, we can be more attentive to them, but Feng has a full load tonight."

"I know," she said, her sweet face contorted in pain. "And who knows if Feng was even told what Captain wanted. Besides, Captain isn't entitled to caviar." She punched her fist in the air. It wasn't easy to accept this hand had to do that. Then the face brightened and the defined eyebrows rose. "Anyway, I told him Feng is a nice man. I made him promise not to tell Richard and Eric what happened."

"I am sure that's not the end of the story."

***

I lifted the curtain and walked down the aisle. All the Stamford passengers were sleeping except for one or two shifting uncomfortably on their seats. The two hostesses entered the toilets on both sides of the cabin when they saw me. I heard flushes, and objects being moved as I reached the end of the zone. They were cleaning and replenishing inside I supposed. I turned left. I ducked under the staircase and walked through the galley which was cold like a mortuary to keep food fresh. I reached starboard and walked slowly up the aisle. I came to the front row, turned around and walked back. I stood behind the last row of the passenger seats which were in front of the folded crew seat. I couldn't sit here and be seen falling asleep. Outside the door porthole, red and blue lights were blinking on the wing in the dark.

A quarter-hour passed, and there was still no sign of Richard and Eric. The weather was calm and the cool cabin vibrated gently in regular spasms like clockwork. The continuous engine roar had a calming effect as footsteps came down the staircase on the port. Feng, jaw set, was walking towards the First Class purposefully.

Instinctively, I rushed to him and asked what he was doing. He said smugly he was getting Connie to be courageous. I wasn't shocked and tried to stop him; but he glanced at me and puckered his face with a stubborn expression. Discouraged, I let him walk into impending disaster.

Immediately, I cursed myself for the moment's weakness. I would get a good view if I stood on the aisle behind the bulkhead curtain, but that was risky. I stood beside door 2 left and waited. Nothing happened for ten minutes. Feng would have to get back before Richard and Eric woke up soon. No crew member had ever done what Feng was doing.

If I stand leftwards, I would lean on the concave door and my body curve with it awkwardly. My head moved slightly to the left. Between the curtain and the centre bulkhead, I could see the First Class galley, the curtain drawn forwards, in the dim light. Nobody inside! I stood straight and looked around. One of the hostesses was throwing nervous glances at me.

"Could I make you a drink?" she asked in a highly-strung voice.

I started. "Tea white, one sugar. Leave it in the galley."

Once she was gone, I leant left again. My face turned right a little and my eyes strained in the First Class direction. Between the bulkhead curtain in front and the aft side of the First Class galley entrance, where the curtain was drawn towards its forward side, Feng in his orange red jacket was standing in the galley. He was talking while Connie was drinking in his words. Her lightly tanned face looked golden in the dim light. The bun perched on her head trembled.

I felt a light tap on my shoulder. I almost jumped.

"Your tea is by the fridge."

I entered the galley and tried to appear normal. The tea had the right milky brown colour, but it tasted bland. I was listening hard for sounds from the First Class cabin. Amidst the purring of engines, creaks of the cabin and the whines of babies from Value, this wasn't easy.

I finished drinking but dared not return to the same spot to continue watching. It would be too soon to do so, and it would arouse the hostesses' suspicion. I lifted the empty cup to my mouth and pretended to be drinking. After a while, I took the ledger book from the bar cart and tried some stock checking. The tension was so unbearable I couldn't focus a moment. I had the recurring feeling Feng was going to get carved and served to First Class passengers. Heart racing, I pushed the cart back and skulked into the cabin.

This time, I walked to the bulkhead and stood behind the curtain. I looked through the gap. Feng was still in the galley, but he was winding up his lecture. Connie was nodding in agreement. I was relieved he would be leaving soon. I was about to turn back to my zone when suddenly he turned around. He was out, and he walked into me.

"Liu!"

I wanted to explain, but a long figure appeared behind him and pulled him back by the neck of his jacket.

"Two of you! Come here!"

***

Richard's voice was high pitched. He was still not in his jacket. We packed into the galley in front of Connie, her eyes wide open. Richard fumbled for the switch but couldn't find it. I pushed it up to "high". He looked fresh in the brightness. There were no signs on his face he had just awoken. In fact, it was glowing with strength.

"I told both of you before: no 'zoning' and you are in First Class. You left your crew to work by themselves without leaders. Do you have a reason?" He began to giggle like a child, as his eyes flashed with hatred.

I didn't know what to say. I hadn't step into First Class, and was only looking from Stamford.

"I came to talk to Connie," Feng said.

"Why should you talk to Connie? What has her life got to do with you?"

"I know you are forcing her against her wishes," Feng stammered.

"Who said? Anyway, this has nothing to do with you. I will complain to management you are not working," Richard screeched.

"She asked me for help."

Connie didn't say anything. She flushed and tears welled up in her eyes. "I only wanted your opinion."

Richard's face lit up. Feng's crumbled as his purposefulness seemed to falter. He was no longer sure he should have been so supportive of Connie, but he also couldn't believe he had been a fool.

"Richard should let you do what you wish. It's your choice. Choose carefully because it's your life," Feng said, maintaining his usual tone of voice.

"Feng, you heard what Connie said. She only wanted an opinion. She asked everyone that, not only you. You too, Liu! Let me advise you both. Just take good care of yourselves. Buck up your work. Both of you are lacking."

I was caught in a difficult situation which was not my business from the beginning. Only the subject of existence concerned me. Still, I had to show support for Feng. He hadn't done anything wrong, after all. And Richard had included me in his wild accusations.

"Feng is fighting for fairness. You've no right …"

"Liu!" Richard lowered his voice. "You are another useless AP. I'm speaking to your Ward Leader."

"Please, gentlemen!" Connie opened and closed her mouth, choking with emotion. "Forgive and forget. Let's get back to work. Richard, please!"

"Are you with me?"

"We're good friends."

"Just that?" Richard whispered, voice shaking.

"Good friends."

Richard held the galley top. He lowered himself onto one of the two containers with the rumpled blankets still on top. He looked at Connie entreatingly.

"Be careful of Howard. He is a killer."

"They say bad things about him. I know Howard very well. He will never do that."

Eric appeared like an ape in a jacket. It knew when to poke its roundish face into the tense galley. Its hair was freshly combed. I could see it had a good sleep. The mouth which had seemed to hold a big bubble inside, was releasing small amounts of air. It had the effect of lightening the atmosphere.

"Passengers are disturbed." Eric sounded as though he was enjoying what was happening. His upper limps swung, and he pulled back the curtain as he left.

They stopped arguing. Richard was slouching again, elbows on his soft thighs. I was grateful for the sudden reprieve from tension.

The First Class passenger outside asked gruffly, "What's going on?"

"Can I get you a drink?" Eric's American accent was faltering.

"Cold water! Put it at my seat while I use the toilet."

We remained silent for some time. I wasn't sure whether Richard and Feng were waiting for the old man to return to his seat, or that they were happy Connie made them even.

"Can we go back, Richard?" I asked.

"Okay, I will talk to you two later," he answered weakly.

***

When the light in Stamford Class was switched on for continental breakfast, Richard came from First

Class and stood at door 2 left. His eyes followed my movements as I collected towels and served juices. He didn't unnerve me as I had stopped caring materially on this flight, but the two hostesses spilt drinks. Richard didn't stay long. He climbed, tiredly, up the staircase.

Smiles sweetened the hostesses' faces. I thought: *Richard is trying to "kill" Feng upstairs and helping him are two colleagues, trying not to make mistakes themselves in front of the CCE.*

We pushed out the meal carts shaking badly in the weather. The coffee and tea pots were half-filled to prevent the hot liquid from spilling. I was on the left aisle while the Cabin Hostess was on the right. Each passenger's table was laid with linen before a pre-dressed tray with a bowl of cut fruit in the centre was served with coffee or tea and a glass of juice. After a few seats, the Galley Hostess offered croissants and hot breads from a basket.

Nothing was happening upstairs as far as I could see. Maybe Richard and Feng had come to an understanding.

We offered cereal and second round beverages, before we collected the trays and gave out towels. Gopal squeezed past the Cabin Hostess' cart to go to the First Class with a package of cigarettes in his hand. (The entire upper deck was designated a non-smoking zone.) We were offering more coffee and tea, and collecting the trays when he returned with a packet of Milo in his hand.

Feng and Richard were up there in the galley when Gopal reached the landing. They were talking angrily to each other. I was sure something nasty was going to happen. I didn't raise my head to look in case Richard noticed it.

"When you have to leave the service, please let me know." It was Feng's angry voice.

"Captain wanted Milo," Gopal retorted.

"You can do it after the service."

"He's not eating. How long does it take to make a Milo?"

"If it doesn't disrupt the service, it's okay. But the service is taking too long and very soon, we are landing. You were missing for fifteen minutes."

"Feng, Captain is the commander," Richard interrupted.

"I respect him as the commander but there are situations …"

"Feng, I'm telling Captain about you. You are recalcitrant."

"Let me complete the service first." Feng said.

I pushed my cart into the galley, before preparing for landing.

***

We ate something quickly. The hostesses didn't talk to me. I guess I was too preoccupied and looked strange and aloof. Eric wanted me to fumigate the cabin for him. I went round with two canisters of pesticide held above my head. When I finished spraying, I went to the First Class and returned the empty cans. My fingertips were almost frozen from holding down the freezing nozzles despite having padded them with serviettes. I didn't expect to see him so anxious.

"Follow me to the upper deck immediately," he said in the flat local accent.

We brushed the curtains aside, ran down the Stamford aisle and pounded up the staircase. Passengers and crew members turned around and stared. Richard and Feng were facing each other in the galley like two hot school boys about to tear each other to pieces.

"I told you time and again to get lost. I won't give you another chance," Richard shouted against the din of the air vents and galley exhausts. His trembling finger was almost poking Feng's nose.

Seeing Richard go crazy probably gave Feng more incentive to fight back. Feng stuck out his chin. "I'm sorry they are suited for each other. They love each other. You have to understand that."

Eric's hand crept above the cart lift. He lifted up the handset and the stubby thumb pressed the cockpit number. "Captain Lobo, please come to the upper deck galley immediately. Big quarrel between the CCE and the AP!"

The upper deck passengers were already turning their heads. The cockpit door opened abruptly, and the oldish Captain limped to the galley, wildly. He was panting when Richard told him what happened. Feng didn't get a chance.

"There's little time before I have to land this aircraft," Captain Lobo said, his long narrow eyes blinking nervously. "Let's get this straight. Feng, I personally think Richard is right about you. You are a nasty fellow and you're recalcitrant. You've no right to interfere in the CCE's affair."

"But Connie asked me for help."

"Bring Connie here!" The Captain's lips quivered.

"I'll get her for you," Gopal said. The young steward put down the jug he was rinsing, on the galley top and ran down the staircase.

"Look, Captain. Howard and Connie are in love. Richard harasses and bullies Connie in the hope she leaves Howard. Who is right and who is wrong, Captain?"

Richard calmed down. "I hold you responsible for the death of Howard's lover. He murdered her. You abetted him."

"Captain, you see how unreasonable this CCE is. Howard didn't kill the woman. That's why he is still flying. And I didn't abet him."

"Captain," Richard said smugly. "He dares to question a commander. I recommend you offload him."

Gopal ran up the staircase. Connie appeared below him, her face white like his shirt.

Captain Lobo said, "Let me speak to Connie before I decide what to do."

At this time, the loud, jarring sound of the microphone being depressed came on. The First Officer's voice was heard announcing the cabin had to be prepared for arrival. The Captain cocked his head to one side, and his hand fumbled in the air.

"I have to get back now but tell me, Connie: did you ask this AP for help in dealing with your Ward Leader?"

"I only wanted his opinion." Her face was red as she stared at the floor.

"That's enough," Captain Lobo said impatiently. "I will call the office later and speak to your director. Now, get ready for landing. It'll be very bumpy with strong winds."

***

After the swaying plane landed and the shaken passengers left, workers rushed in like insects to prepare the aircraft for the return. We had to leave quickly so that we wouldn't be in their way. We locked up some compartments and walked into the airport with our bags on trolleys or carried by tired hands.

Feng looked exhausted like any of us, but Richard was worse. His greasy forehead shone in the morning light, and the thinning hair clung to it like plaster. A few crew members vomited during the landing and looked pale. The crew kept away from Feng. Richard, Eric and the steward looked like inspectors in control, walking together behind.

Long queues from different flights waited at customs. Muzzled dogs on leash sniffed for drugs and explosives. The crew had to queue with the passengers. Feng placed his bag on the conveyor belt, and Gopal stooped to watch the screen. Richard and Eric saw what happened and giggled among themselves.

Outside the airport, the autumn weather was nice and warm.

We shared the bus with the pilots. Captain Lobo sat in front with Richard and Eric, and his two officers. The two officers wore sunglasses. (They weren't cabin crew members.) I took a seat next to Feng at the back. Everyone was quiet and solemn. Soon most of us were nodding and swaying. Thirty minutes later, we arrived at the hotel. I was relieved to be free till the next morning.

When I woke up, I phoned Feng. I thought he needed someone to talk to, but he didn't answer my call. Maybe, he had a girlfriend here too. Maybe he needed to be alone.

***

The next morning, after the call time at ten, I thought: *Feng is okay! If he is offloaded, he would've called.* But I dared not call him to make sure. I hope to see him in uniform later, signing in for duty, this time, in the main deck Stamford Class.

I put on my uniform, had some biscuits and took the lift down to the lobby. On one side was the reception counter; on the other the main restaurant. Some locals loitered in the large area after their buffet breakfast. Nearly the whole set of crew were on the sofas in the centre, huddled in groups as though they dreaded the flight but were even more afraid to be late. A hostess checked out at the counter. I didn't expect it when Peter Lim, walked up to me in uniform. The AP wasn't with me on the flight to Melbourne. I thought, maybe, he had reported sick and was a passenger going home.

"Liu, what happened? I got called up," he said.

"Called up to replace whom?"

"Don't know! I heard someone was offloaded."

My head began to swim. My legs felt weak. I walked to the nearest empty seat with a view of the lifts and sat down.

The lift doors opened and Richard, his face beaming, walked out with Eric. There was a spring in Richard's gait. The other lift opened too, and Gopal swaggered out to meet Richard. All the three men were smiling as if they were congratulating each other. Then the steward left to tell everybody what happened. Eric came and told me what Feng was expected to do.

Connie and Feng were still not at the lobby, other than the fresh pilots. (Captain Lobo and his pilots would leave later, in the evening). The Flight Record was passed around on a clip board, and the crew signed their names next to their work positions. A note reminding them of the severe consequences of insubordination was clipped on top. I didn't know how to break the news to Feng. I wasn't concerned with Connie. I was only worried about the humanist who was offloaded.

Connie and Feng walked out of the lift. Connie was quite tall for a girl and nearly the same height as Feng. She was very beautiful and her fit shapely figure moved gracefully in the hugging sarong kebaya. Feng still looked purposeful. I walked up and pulled Feng to one side as the pilots arrived. He looked at me as if he knew what I was going to say.

"Feng, I want …"

"Say anything. You know I can take any shit."

"You won't be working today. They gave you a Value seat."

A smile appeared on his lips and spread to his eyes. He said, "I think that could be what I need." Then the smiles faded, and he gave a cynical laugh. "And what do I do? Throw my uniform away?"

"No, you still have to clear Immigration in uniform. Your name is on the General Declaration. They've not given you a ticket. In the cabin, you can change into civilian. You have not been sacked. You can still fight the case and clear your name."

"Fight what? I don't want to fly anymore. I thought about it the whole of last night. Serving passengers is no longer a joy."

We had to leave the hotel. We climbed up the bus heaving heavy hand luggage. There were two vacant seats together in the middle. I asked him to get in first, but he walked to the back of the bus and sat alone.

Everyone was whispering to each other, their unsmiling eyes moving within the small area in front of themselves. They sympathised with Feng, but were unwilling to show it out of fear. Eric told the pilots why Feng was being offloaded. Richard was leaning towards Connie's impassive face, trying hard to make her smile. The steward had an omniscient shine on his face.

At the airport, Feng walked behind the crew till we cleared Immigration and Customs. Then he wandered off and later, boarded the flight with passengers.

***

I was working in the upper deck, too busy to know what went on below, in Value.

After take-off, when lunch service completed, I went down to look for Feng. As expected, the Value cabin was full of passengers packed neatly like helpless cattle. They were given food and drink they paid for, so they could pretend to be happy. Each one had a strap to keep themselves from harm's unpredictable ways. Lunch was over and except for two or three trays, the cabin had been cleared. I found Feng seated at the last row next to the aisle in front of the toilets. They had arranged for him to sit there and even assigned Gopal to look after him.

His eyes were closed, the lines between his eyebrows squeezed into a tight knot. The air was stuffy with a powerful smell of air fresheners. A long line of passengers stood beside him, taking turns to use the toilets. He sat upright with folded arms, as the passenger in front of him had reclined her seat. The low end of the seat back squashed his knees while the upper part was pushing his face.

"Feng!"

The eyelids lifted slowly. He murmured as he raised his hand. "Leave me alone."

Gopal arrived with an innocent smile on his lean face and a serving tray on his hand. He looked like an athlete holding a trophy.

"Thanks for waiting!" The words came mockingly out of his thick, wide lips. "Passengers who ask for cookies are told there is none left. But for you, it's different." He took a plate full of sweet biscuits from the tray and laid it neatly on Feng's table. Then he positioned a tea and a serviette at its sides. "By the way, thanks for your help in giving up your meal."

"Not enough trays! Surely you have spare main meals and bread," I said impatiently.

"Eric said those are only for crew," he said coolly, his hooknose in the air.

"I have extra trays and meals in the Stamford Class. Why didn't you ask me for them?"

"Richard said Value passengers are to be given Value food. Stamford meals are meant for Stamford and First Class passengers."

"Just get out of here," Feng said gruffly. "And bring your dirty food with you!"

Gopal put the biscuits and tea back on his tray. He walked back with his head held high.

"I will get you some food from Stamford Class," I said.

"No, I don't want to get you into trouble. I had a hamburger before checking out, so I am all right."

"But you've to eat. That hamburger was hours ago. I'll talk to Captain."

"Don't bother. I am in no mood to eat."

I knew him enough to know he meant it. "Maybe later, before landing, I bring you some food."

"Ask me before you bring it. I am telling you I don't want to eat. It's only this seat. It can't be reclined!"

"Those bastards! I'll fix them for you. Richard and Eric were sleeping in the First Class yesterday. Connie and the other JP saw it."

"No use! Connie will never testify against Richard, and the JP will never help you. No cabin crew member will help you at the expense of themselves. Don't bother. I am resigning. I have prepared a letter which I will give to Eric. And the Director, I had issues with him before: he couldn't do anything, and he told me many times to leave the Company if I was not happy. Now, he has his wish."

I understood what he was saying. Feng was a changed man. I guessed he had become like me. At least a little!

"You better be sure. Those who left the airline: ninety percent regretted it."

"I've made up my mind. I have already travelled the world. I think it's time to leave, before I get stuck here forever. I still love flying, but this job is meaningless. It was I who was a fool; not those crew. They never mind wearing fake smiles which they think are real."

I knew he was right. I also knew he was sad to leave. I could see it in his eyes as they were wet with tears.

"Don't hand in the letter yet. You may want to change your mind."

***

I came down to Value again to see him before the flight landed. He looked happier and even gave me one of those purposeful smiles. He still refused to eat, so I didn't bring him the food from Stamford Class. He said he had handed in the resignation letter. I was really saddened by what he did, but I had really expected it. And deep inside, I knew he would be the man who laughed last.

"We won't be sharing transport. Let me call you when you reach home. I'll go to see you tonight."

He put on his headset and didn't answer. I let him drift away and returned upstairs to close my bar.

***

After the flight landed, I wasted no time and got home. I phoned him a few times, but he didn't answer my calls.

Chapter 13
The State of Mind

Before I fly off each time, there are personal matters to attend and complete. Something usually happens when I'm away, and I can't do anything about it. I sort it out on my return, but it's often too late. Offices could even be closed, there is urgent stuff, or I forgot to sort that very matter out. I lose momentum built up when I leave. On my return, I can't get it back even when I try hard. Flying plays havoc on my body too. I try to sleep before flying at night. When I arrive in a city in the morning, I'm tired and sleepy. I become a zombie when I try to keep up. I waste much of my life trying to sleep and not getting it. And there are worries about exposure to heavy radiation and lack of oxygen at thirty thousand feet; not to mention radiation from security equipment and eating affected food. I've the feeling I'm completely warped.

I'm leaving tomorrow on a sixteen-day flight. I've the sick feeling I will leave something behind and be affected by it.

This morning, I went to the bank to top up my current account and withdraw some cash. At the brokerage, I paid for shares bought a few days ago, with a cheque. Then I went to the money changer in the city centre to buy US and Hong Kong dollars, and the supermarket for stuff I would need.

If I didn't bring something I need for the stopovers, I would live with the consequences for the whole trip. If I found it overseas, I would've spent lots of time and more money on it. I couldn't decide whether it would be a gain or loss to go through that. There would be material loss, but in terms of knowledge and experience, I wasn't sure. If there was overall loss, how much would it be? The more I thought, the more convoluted the issue was.

By evening, I felt more than desperate. I was in no mood to talk to family members at home. I slunk to a corner and ate a tasteless dinner alone.

The fact is I feel I don't belong anywhere. I am an unwanted orphan or a street urchin. Everything seems to have stepped back away from me and my reach.

I leave for Hong Kong tomorrow with a motley set of crew. I don't even know who they are. Most of them would be strangers, anyway. Two days later, we fly to Honolulu, stay for a few days, and stop at San Francisco. We then return to Honolulu, Hong Kong and finally home.

I've been to these wonderful cities, but each time I left, they turned their faces and didn't want to know me anymore. I've not left the island but, of course, it knows I'm going to leave. It already shut its shops and offices because I've finished business with it. Workers have removed appurtenances and kept them behind doors which were then tightly closed. They even shut the windows and claimed they needed rest when I called.

At this time, the aloof city eagerly awaits my departure with almost empty streets.

***

I just arrived at the terrace house. A canvas canopy was erected over the brightly lit patio and car porch. Crew members of all ranks are whispering politely, huddled here tonight. There are one or two pilots and even a manager; and the family's relatives and friends.

People seated around wooden tables nearby, look at me with ceremonious welcome, nodding solemn heads. I pull an empty chair from a table and sit with those on my right.

"Roland was very hardworking, you know," the Indian-looking Malay they are calling Kassim, says. He has thick mascara on his eyes and a hive of curls on his head. "That Ramesh was harassing him from Hong Kong to Honolulu. You know Ramesh *lah*. Another Purser who dies for girls!"

"Is Roland like this?" the middle-aged Baba flicks his hand and asks. His face is full of pimple marks smoothed and whitened with cosmetic. "I hadn't met him, but I realised he was very good-looking once I saw him today. What a waste!" His flexible hand latches onto his slender waist as the elbow thrusts like an angry wedge. "Next time I meet *chee hong* Ramesh, I'll tell the cunt maniac off."

"*Shh!* Leslie. This is a serious occasion. Don't talk like that." Kassim blinks like he usually does when talking to handsome men. He continues in his hoarse, feminine voice: "Passengers and crew all like Roland, but Ramesh you know lah, is a slave driver to guys. He scolded the poor steward throughout the flight. He shouted at him in front of the passengers."

"Ramesh was a Steward when I was his JP." Leslie's other hand lands on the other side so there are two similar wedges. "Very disorganised in galley work and had no priorities. Once he forgot to turn on the ovens after takeoff and tried to serve lukewarm meals. Luckily, I found out or else I would've been in deep shit. At the end, we landed with many trays uncollected."

"We were batch boys during Basic Class." Kassim pouts his lips and stamps his foot. "He didn't know anything, but was a super 'balls carrier'. He was caught for cheating during a test and went on his knees to beg. And the stupid instructor forgave him." Kassim glares into space before making the act of spitting. "*Pui!*"

"What a sickening character!"

"There are many like him among us. Roland used to say they should be made to fly together and do what they love to each other throughout. Anyway, in Honolulu, the crew was checking into the hotel when some girls suspected something wrong. Roland couldn't remember their names. The trouble is one of those girls brought this out only tonight."

"Has he got good memory?" Leslie asked, interested about Roland.

"Oh yes and an unusually sharp tongue like yours! He was paranoid about his weight. He jogged a lot. We went for coffee together often. Roland was always very generous. He had expensive tastes, and he dressed very well. Last year, we went to Italy. He bought two bags full of Gucci and Prada stuff. He was a shrewd investor. I should have bought those shares he recommended. Now, I regret whenever I see rich people. He was just a JP, but he owned houses in Thailand and London. His sisters showed me some of his Rolex watches this afternoon. They were diamond studded. Unfortunately, they were all left behind. Roland never stopped loving this job. That's why the sisters decided he should be in uniform for the last time. He was missing during checkout. They went to his room and found him."

Kassim sobs and continues. "It is so sad. The room stank. He was still in uniform and his face was grey. The coroner said it was stroke, and that he left soon after checking in. Stress *lah!* And not enough sleep. I want to slap that Purser on his *chee hong* face."

"Don't be crude, sister. Have some respect for Roland." Leslie helps Kassim wipe his tears with tissues he took effeminately from Kassim's LV handbag.

I get up and walk to the makeshift table with the money box on it. A lady in a white blouse and black pants sits with a notebook and a pen. I hand over two ten-dollar notes and tell her how sorry I am. She recorded the amount against my name and gives me a red string. Then I walk solemnly behind the altar to the open coffin.

Roland is relaxed as though lying in a First Class seat. He is in his well-pressed white shirt and sky-blue jacket, a crisp bow tie affixed to his neck. His fresh-cut hair is short and neat, abiding by company standard. The embalmer has done a good job. The corpse smiles and looks ready to rise and serve.

A soft look suggests he was gay or perhaps bisexual. I worked with him when he began flying, and I swear he was then one hundred percent straight. They're right to say Cabin Crew is a conversion class for closet gays. He was definitely good-looking and would look very masculine had he wanted to. No wonder Leslie was full of praise for him.

One thinks of the past, wrings the hands and feels sorry for pains they once inflicted on Roland. They congratulate themselves if they had done something for him before he died. A respect and sympathy for death transcends seniority and raises them. They adjust to each other's level as old feuds and grudges are left behind, at least for the night. Hostesses terrified of Kassim's and Leslie's picking and bitching, are relaxed and friendly with the gay Pursers tonight.

A sense of peace and unity lurks beneath the ostensible grief pervading funerals and wakes. Death frees Roland from delusions and miseries. It helps free me from the worries about tomorrow's trip.

***

It reminds me that when my father collapsed and died in front of me not long ago, there was confusion over what I should or not have done. The subsequent question was what I should do when he was alive. I wanted to be more caring towards him since my mother died, and had told myself to learn more about my father and his peers before they passed away. Day after day, I didn't change, and day after day, I told myself I had to. But the consuming question remained what else should have been done to save him when I was first told of his condition by the maid. Why did I give up so easily? How was I sure he was dead? What had the thing to do with it? Grief eventually emerged stronger than the confusion. Soon, I realised grief was better than the daily struggles with the thing. Calm and acceptance were slowly felt beneath the grief. I saw there is nothing bad about death. Yet, all I saw was nothing.

Once I realised I was focused on grieving, the thoughts I struggled with daily fought for their right to my mind. I fought unsuccessfully to return. I found myself dangling between two worlds. In fact, grief lost as I couldn't grieve anymore. I was desperate and helpless. It was less painful, yet more painful. It was a deeper and a different pain not being able to grieve. The ambiguity tore my consciousness and wrung my heart as the funeral proceeded. It existed, spread over me for some time and gradually dissipated.

This ambiguity hung somewhere, quiet and untouched till tonight.

***

You can burn Roland's body and break the ashes into atoms; smash the atoms in an accelerator and can't find him. Cut open his brain, palpate the muscles, dissect the heart, filter the drained blood – if X-rays don't show. You can analyse his mind and feel for the soul, scream or shout at it and still can't find him. If you cried, you wouldn't find him. Whatever they say about Roland, you can't find him. You can ask for his personal records from the office and find nothing. Shred the notes, and you will find nothing that is him.

I'm feeling better now. I'm ready to leave home for more than two weeks. There is still time tonight to read up relevant notes for the flight before I sleep. I wave goodbye, reluctantly.

The bus stop is not far to walk to. Soon I'm standing next to the post in front of the "five-foot way". I'm normally sensible at bus stops, or else the buses will pass me by. But now, I don't feel the importance of not missing it. To tell the truth, I'm grateful for the chance to be forgotten. The faces around don't know me, and no lands claim me. They don't care what happens to me; and, what I do. I'm as good as a rag on the floor or a smell in the air.

The object comes swiftly to the pavement to mop up the forlorn crowd. Men, women and children scramble for the crowded door, in the middle, with worried eyes. The vehicle halts noisily, far ahead of the stop, and spews black smoke with a powerful smell. Passengers clutch their belongings as they drop to disembark. I join the rush to hold some support and step on board. The bus pulls away, leaving disappointed faces with mouths agape.

I don't feel the bus is providing a service tonight, or that I've to pay for the trip. The rectangular object is a jerky box with rollers, not a vehicle. It's an existent within existence, and I'm conscious of the existent.

I climb two more steps and stand on the floor. Passengers step down to disembark at different stops. I push my way slowly into the packed crowd.

I'm conscious of my existence. It is both sweet and sickening. It also has the qualities of being unnecessary and stubborn, but it's never unimportant. It is, after all, existence.

A pressure of light, the existent exists among the sea of impersonal faces. Someone gets up, and the existent squeezes sideways past a pair of legs in front of the aisle seat. It lowers itself onto the empty space and spreads – transparent and lucid – against the sidewall. It rattles when the glass windows, with reflections of faces and lights, rattle. It is aware of the existence of warmth on the seat left by the previous existent.

But "I" is missing. *Where am I?* "I" which I don't know what it is. "I" appears, flickers in midair and dwindles before my very eyes.

The form in a white shirt with epaulettes, enters the consciousness and speaks in Hokkien: "How much you paying?" A canvas pouch in front of the waist hangs from the back of a damp neck. A napkin with dark lines, attached to the inside of the collar with paper clips, absorbs sweat. The form balances on shifting objects. One hand vibrates with the bus, clutches a board banded with stacks of colourful tickets; as the other, holding a single-hole puncher, flips the device deftly and squeezes.

The light figure on the seat, the consciousness recognises is Liu, looks up and hands over three round objects. It takes in return a flat rectangle, after a hole was punched on it. The figure slips the paper into the front of its shirt.

A thought enters. Kassim is weeping and Leslie wipes Kassim's face tenderly. The vivid scene lingers for a while and disappears. Then a less vivid scene as Kassim bitches and scolds passengers, complete with artistic gestures, and the others roar with laughter. Trains of thoughts appear in a long transparent line: Crews are prone to illnesses and problems. They get strokes and heart attacks at a young age, cancer and diabetes; and the gays get AIDS. They gamble their allowances away, get drunk and indulge in sex. Something else: they shoplift and get caught. Oh yes! They need shrinks' help. So far – touch wood – the planes were not involved in any crash or ditching! Buy the share!

A voice squeaks in the wilderness: *Enjoy your flight tomorrow. It's long, but just think: you get paid to see the world.* The "I" reenters, it refuses to go away, it gets heavy and important – and suddenly, I'm frightened.

***

At home, I put the finishing touches into packing my bags. Roland's face in the large colour photo in front of the coffin lingers in my mind. In two days, the picture would be the only image left of him, and his powdery remains would be no different from others'.

I sit at my desk and pull open the drawer. I remove a frayed folder and take an old poster (about twelve inches times eight) from it. On the flat piece of paper in black and white, a lone negro is walking alongside low warehouses and piles of cargoes. He isn't lonely. He is laughing to himself.

Slowly, I remember, once – a long time ago – I found the picture on a tray mat, lining a CJ tray, far away in an orangey restaurant in California. I'm flying to a nearby city, in the state tomorrow. In San Francisco, I could go to the CJ restaurant at Market Street, opposite my hotel, to see if copies of the same photo are on the trays. Maybe, it made a return due to popular demand. Maybe this time, they are copies of the early copy. But so what! Even if they are somewhat less clear. A return is more possible than finding a needle in a haystack.

The photo is frayed and yellowish at the edges, it was stretched and compressed many times, and there are marks and brown stains. There is even a thin scratch across the dark young face above the cobblestone street. The poster was handled often. Too often, I think! But the face is still laughing, and there is no doubt this was the person on that mat long ago. His appearance and his youth are unchanged. The identity is the same.

Thousands of the same pictures were once created out of nothingness and distributed all over the world with the help of modern transportation. At first, it appeared in restaurants, then in bags and finally in homes where they were found in drawers like mine. Of these, many were destroyed and disappeared from existence. Some pictures of the Negro, (besides this one in front of me), still exist no doubt, seemingly not getting older by the day, only deteriorating inexorably, but it will last many more lifetimes.

These paper Negroes came into existence one day, when someone lifted his camera out of quick thinking to create the Negro in another world. Maybe, he had been thinking he himself was born into the wrong side of the world. He yearned to exist in a picture on flat paper. He thought he could choose his friends for the picture and even wear his favourite shirt. Then, the piece of paper could slip between the secure pages of a thick book with hard covers. His world would become unchanging and time stand still. What he likes would be with him forever. He couldn't do this for himself, so he decided to do it for someone else.

He is lucky because someone, who feels like him in a way, is thinking of him in this space-time world. This person is sitting over a cluttered desk somewhere near the Equator, lost in troubling thoughts before leaving on a long trip around the world. Inside the poor guy's head, dripping with perspiration on the hot humid night, random images of him are made.

This guy's sufferings are much worse than his because this guy tried everything. This guy even thought of how to secure a permanent place inside reflections. He didn't know whether he was making headway when he tried to do so, in front of glass and mirrors, not only at home, but in aircraft toilets and hotel rooms as well. It's even more ephemeral than his present world, he finally admitted. He thought of standing in front of temples and becoming a statue, like someone carved out of stone; or getting mummified upon death and hopefully, kept after that in a museum. But he felt such an existence was not satisfying either, and besides, it was beyond his control.

In fact, he lives on the wrong side of everything. He feels lopsided like a tree, looking perfectly normal, standing next to a building or a road. Its serpentine roots have squeezed themselves to one side to fit the concrete structures, and its leaves and branches are constantly sprayed with pesticide and pruned to suit bloodsucking humans. Wrong side of history, wrong side of human prejudices, wrong side of life! Wrong side in existence or inexistence! Misaligned preferences!

He thinks of others and what they're going through often; what were the obstacles they overcame or still have to overcome which no one knows except themselves. But he knows no one would think about him the same way. No one knows how much he suffers; no one sees the terrible obstacles strewn in his path. No one cares whether he overcomes those obstacles or not. No one would believe those unfortunate mistakes could have taken place even if he tells them.

Confusing emotions run wild in his broken heart as he asks what in the photographer's mind caused the decision to press the button which sealed the fates of two persons.

I remember I once imagined: One cool morning, many years ago, in the harbour of Los Angeles, famed as The City of Angels, a man was walking with a rectangular box. It was quite heavy in a stylish leather case, hanging from his neck, and he was thinking of making a name for himself. He had hoped people would think when they saw the picture (he was going to make), and say: *the man who took this photo: he must be a genius*. He was wondering what to capture on the nice breezy late morning, bereft of ideas, a confused look on his face, when he saw this Negro walking by himself next to tasteless buildings, wooden boxes and brown sacks of food. There was nothing remarkable about the man. He was neither handsome nor ugly, but he was laughing heartily, a beautiful laugh bursting from the centre of his soul – out of nature. Without a second thought, before it was too late, the man unsnapped the box, not bothered with the click he heard and let the cover flap down. He saw the Negro on the square screen on top of his box (a tiny moving figure) and everything was all right, and quickly pressed the button. All was done in that split of a second – the decision which brought him glory forever or he would be forgotten.

He wasn't sure he would achieve his aim, at first. If not, he hoped only to earn a few dollars. He submitted the picture to a local newspaper and waited. They weren't interested in it and didn't even have the courtesy to return the photograph. He told himself there were people more frustrated. After a long time, one day out of desperation, he tried his luck at the State Photography Competition. He only got a consolation prize, but that was really good enough for him. He never expected it when one day, an advertising agency traced him to his dilapidated apartment in downtown Los Angeles, where he was struggling with rent and eating supermarket takeaway every day – and a woman asked if he was interested in big money.

If I can do something like this (and get people to think of me) or get someone to write about me as I wrote about Feng and Ramesh, or if I could get myself into a picture which lasts, I would exist in another world, in the glory of people's minds, perhaps in immortality.

***

I've forgotten Isness again. It doesn't do anything. It doesn't care.

But it is everything!

Epilogue

It is 2009. The airline is one of the largest carriers in the world, and Cabin Crew itself has gone through big changes. It's now an exception for a member to be promoted at the speed and ease when the airline was shooting upwards in its growth trajectory. Animal bitching among the crew members was ruthless and senseless then, but now it's the relentless productivity drive and the nasty competition for promotion and a good record with the Company, that is wearing them thin.

Richard's star had been falling ever since his brother-in-law was deployed to another division as part of the Company's routine rotation of talent. The CCE job was on the chopping board for some time, since it became obvious to everyone it was a waste of money. The decision was made to retrench non-performing staff, and offer all the CCEs and some older colleagues early retirement packages following a quarterly loss for the first time in the Company's history. Reluctant to leave, but fearing the adverse consequences of defying management, Richard retired and joined a few CCEs and a local businessman to start a consultancy firm which airlines could tap for advice on inflight service. It closed as swiftly as it started, and he found himself working as a property agent, then a security guard and finally a taxi driver.

Howard and Connie are happily married but have no children. Howard's case is still open, but no one suspects him of killing his ex-lover any more. He had also taken a retirement package and now lives with Connie in China, where he is employed by an airline to train its cabin crew.

Ramesh is still a bachelor and isn't working. He ploughs about his neighbourhood on clutches whenever he needs exercise; otherwise, he is seen racing on his motorised wheelchair in one of the air-conditioned shopping malls in the sweltering island.

What led to his leaving the airline, some say, was karma. He was counting ghost money with gusto on his lustful face one day, when he walked into an opened manhole at Dam Square. A prostitute saw him fall (luckily!) and ran out of her cubicle in her panties, shouting to passersby for help. They called an ambulance which brought him to the same hospital he was once warded. This time, though, he was covered in sewage and smelling of faeces. Doctors made the difficult decision to save his broken leg, and he was allowed to stay in Hotel Okura after discharge.

He was recovering and waiting for the doctor's permission to fly home, and his allowances were getting bloated because he wasn't working. He realised that, and was happily calculating his real money when the station manager called to say the Airline would be boarding him out medically. (The Company's astute panel of doctors had concluded Ramesh would not recover from his serious injury to ever work again, even if he could keep his leg.) Not even the compensation of a hundred thousand dollars could console him, and he was heard sobbing by himself, in his room, that night.

It turned out the Company's doctors were right. On arriving home on the flight, the same leg broke again at the airport despite the fact there was no incident. At the hospital this time, doctors removed the lower half of his left leg.

Only Gopal is still flying with the airline. The tall man with deep set, supercilious eyes and big hungry lips is now a fearsome AP and a trainer. Although his work on board has repeatedly been questioned, everyone agrees he has talent. He has always been very good picking the right balls to polish and doing it well, even as he destroys others.

Feng lives in a big house with his wife and four children. They're a happy family. I'm glad he has chosen not to follow the monkey-follow-monkey campaign to have two or less children in the island. When the boys and girls were growing up, husband and wife took turns to provide care and guidance. An accountant, his wife is supportive and respects him as an individual, just as he respects her and others.

Feng owns and runs a few medium-sized consultation companies which are generally doing well. He still lives on principles though I'm not sure if he compromises a little, nowadays. He is as optimistic as ever. These are some of the very traits which brought him success, but that doesn't mean he has the truth with him; so while he exudes confidence and people now admires him like I always do, I don't envy him.

I haven't changed much, but I'm largely at peace. My predictions and worse fears came true again and again. History is repetitive when it seems I'm still unable to benefit from being right. I can forgive myself for the occasional feeling I only lose.

That is why, since school, I have an aversion to success. It seems failure is bad, but success has more to lose. Regret fascinates and hobbles me, keeping in place the cycles of insight and loss, but it's now controlled.

Once in a while, I encounter Isness. That, the implications and the knowledge I don't have much time left in reality, are what I am thankful for.

– The End –

ABOUT THE AUTHOR

He seems to be part of the background most of the time, barely someone who stands out from the crowd. If he impresses, you won't remember him after that.

Appendix I

Crew Ranks in *Inexorable States of Mind*

Cockpit Crew
Captain
Commander of the flight
First Officer

Cabin Crew
Purser
Overall cabin crew-in-charge
Assistant Purser (AP)
Junior Purser (JP)
Steward or Hostess

Appendix II

The Three Classes in the Cabin

First Class with the biggest seats

Stamford Class with the larger seats

Value Class with the bulk of the passengers

INEXORABLE